Open Learning Guide 8

How to Find and Adapt Materials and Select Media

Roger Lewis and Nigel Paine

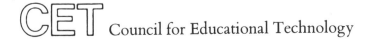
Council for Educational Technology

Published and distributed by the Council for Educational Technology, 3 Devonshire Street, London W1N 2BA

First published 1986
ISBN 0 86184–154–9

Lewis, Roger, *1944–*
    How to find and adapt materials and select media. — (Open learning guide; 8)
    1. Text-books — Authorship   2. Distance education
    I. Title. II. Paine, Nigel III. Council for Educational Technology for the United Kingdom IV. Series
    371.3'12   LB3045.5

ISBN 0–86184–154–9

Printed in Great Britain by H Charlesworth & Co Ltd
254 Deighton Road
Huddersfield HD2 1 JJ

How to Find and Adapt Materials and Select Media

Contents

Preface

Since 1975 the Council for Educational Technology has been continuously involved in the development of open-learning systems. The first stages of this work concentrated on 'non-advanced further education' and enabled the Council to make a major contribution to the National Extension College's 'FlexiStudy' system and other early developments, and incidentally to provide much advice and practical help in the form of publications and training workshops to lecturers who were finding their way into the new field of open learning. This experience (allied to that of the Open University) helped to provide the foundation upon which the 'Open Tech' programme (Manpower Services Commission) and PICKUP initiative (Department of Education and Science) are built, has led to the much more flexible approach now being taken by the Business and Technician Education Council and other validating bodies, and is recognized by the contract given to the Council by MSC to provide a training and support unit for Open Tech projects.

Maintaining the momentum of its work in open learning, the Council has moved into the fields of supported self-study in secondary schools and informal adult learning. In all this work over the past nine years, the Council has benefited from the cooperation and personal experience of an increasingly large group of experienced specialists in open learning and has, through its publications, attempted to make this experience available to lecturers, trainers and teachers who found themselves confronted with the need to get involved in open-learning methods.

This new series of Open Learning Guides is a further move in making the accumulated experience of those who have developed open-learning methods in the United Kingdom available to newcomers to the field. The series editor, Roger Lewis, has taken a lead in developments both through his work for the National Extension College and through his involvement from the beginning with the Council's own work. The drafts of the Guides have been commented on and improved by a process of consultation with several experts in the open-learning network, with the intention that the result will be a series of books which are directly helpful to those in industry, the professions, and adult, further and higher education who are called upon to develop and run open-learning schemes.

Norman Willis
Assistant Director
Council for Educational Technology
April 1984

Introduction

Introduction

THE OPEN-LEARNING GUIDES
This series of books is intended as a practical help to people setting up open-learning schemes whether in education or training. The advice is deliberately aimed across the whole range of schemes and levels. The structure of the series is as follows.

WHAT IS OPEN LEARNING?

OPEN LEARNING IN ACTION: CASE STUDIES

MANAGEMENT	TUTORING	LEARNING MATERIAL
HOW TO DEVELOP AND MANAGE AN OPEN-LEARNING SCHEME	HOW TO TUTOR AND SUPPORT LEARNERS	HOW TO FIND AND ADAPT MATERIALS AND CHOOSE MEDIA
		HOW TO HELP LEARNERS ASSESS THEIR PROGRESS: HOW TO WRITE OBJECTIVES, SELF-ASSESSMENT QUESTIONS AND ACTIVITIES
		HOW TO COMMUNICATE WITH THE LEARNER
		HOW TO MANAGE THE PRODUCTION PROCESS

The Guides thus cover the three main parts of most schemes: a management system, a tutorial support system and learning materials. Each book stands on its own but there are many areas of overlap and reference is made to other volumes in the series. In particular you are recommended to consult Volume 1, *Open Learning in Action*, the case studies volume, as you use this text.

All the volumes except *Open Learning in Action* contain open-learning features. These include

— objectives
— quiz sections which act as summaries
— activities to enable you to apply your learning to your work
— checklists to guide you whilst working through the activities
— job aids to use in running your scheme
— frequent examples and references to show how the ideas have been applied in particular cases.

These features are indicated in the text by introductory symbols to make them easily recognizable. Key words for this volume are defined in the Glossary (see Part Three).

WHAT THIS BOOK COVERS
This book falls mainly into two distinct parts. The first deals with finding and using existing packages; the second, with choice of media. A third part contains the job aids and checklists for both parts together with a common booklist and glossary.

Part One. How to find and adapt materials for use in open learning
Most schemes of open learning use a package. A crucial question is: where does this package come from? A surprisingly large number of people assume that the only route is to develop their own. In fact there is a range of choices including the following:

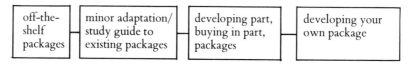

This book concentrates on the options on the left. We show you how to find existing packages. These may already be in open-learning form, or they may be adapted to suit open learning. We cover

— the advantages of using ready-made packages
— how to find packages
— how to evaluate packages
— how to prepare a 'study guide' for resources that may not themselves be in open-learning form.

Objectives
As a result of your work on this part of the book you should be able to carry out the following activities for your own scheme:

— search wholeheartedly for a ready-made package

— evaluate the packages you find
— adapt packages that are basically suitable for use as they stand
— write a study guide to enable other resources to be used by your learners.

Part Two. How to select media
The second part of the book looks at another question that will concern anyone planning an open-learning scheme: which media should we use for the package? It includes sections on

— the principles to use when you are choosing a medium
— the characteristics and uses of a wide range of media.

Objectives
As a result of your work on this part of the book you should be able to carry out the following activities for your own scheme:

— use a systematic approach to choosing media
— weigh up the advantages and disadvantages of a range of possible media
— choose media that suit your learners, and their circumstances, bearing in mind the resources you have available.

You can find more detailed contents and related objectives in the introductions to the various sections contained within each part of the book.

ACKNOWLEDGEMENTS
A team of readers very helpfully commented on this book in draft. The readers were:

John Coffey   Phil Race
Rob Littlejohn   Frances Robertson
Gaye Manwaring   Doug Spencer
Clive Neville   Bob Windsor

Dave Greenfield (the Open University), Clive Jeffries (the National Extension College), Keith Roach (University College, Cardiff) and Quentin Whitlock (Dean Associates) all offered expert comment on Part Two of this book. The authors acknowledge their interest and help whilst remaining responsible for any errors. They would also like to thank Jane Burton (Council for Educational Technology) for her help with the section on Videotex.
     The authors are grateful to Janet Bollen of NEC for her administrative and moral support, and to Clive Neville (Project Manager), Joan Welch and Muriel Brooks for seeing the botk through the final stages of production and publication.

Part One. How to Find and Adapt Materials for Use in Open Learning

Section One. Using What Exists

CONTENTS

INTRODUCTION

This section is divided into four parts. The first part summarizes the features open-learning packages usually include. How many of these are necessary in your own case? The second part outlines three routes to getting the right package for your scheme. These are (in ascending order of cost and complexity): buy a ready-made package off the shelf; write a study guide to resources that have not themselves been designed for use in open-learning or may be in open-learning form but are not right for you; or write your own package from scratch.

The next part reinforces the difficulties of the third route — writing your own package — and gives examples of current developments in which open-learning schemes are delivering existing packages.

This section ends with a job aid which you can use for selecting your package and for charting your route through this book.

Objectives

O

After working through this section you should be able to carry out the following activities in your own scheme:

— decide what kind of package you need
— use the quickest and most economical route to get this package.

THE ROLE OF THE PACKAGE IN OPEN LEARNING

Volume 6, *How to Communicate with the Learner*, describes the support elements that an open-learning package should contain. These are the open-learning equivalents of the help the teacher or trainer provides in a well-run conventional class. They carry out the functions of:

— arousing interest
— making objectives clear
— structuring the content
— giving practice

9

— attending to the difficult and unfamiliar
— establishing two-way communication.

(You should turn to Section One of Volume 6, *How to Communicate with the Learner,* for more detail.) These functions are embodied in the package in various ways, eg,

— objectives
— self-assessment questions (and related, eg, exercises, self-check questions, review questions)
— activities
— feedback on questions and activities
— informal style
— examples
— checklists
— job aids
— summary sections.

These are discussed in detail in Volume 6, *How to Communicate with the Learner.*

Your own requirements for a package will depend on a variety of things, for example:

— the target learners
— any tutoring or other support you will be providing
— the nature of the subject/skill
— where the learning will be taking place
— practical aspects (eg, cost and availability of the package).

Volume 5, *How to Design and Manage an Open-Learning Scheme,* goes into more detail on these course design issues.

Activity

Decide which of the following features are most important, and which one(s) you might leave out and why:

— objectives
— self-assessment questions (and related, eg, exercises, self-check questions, review questions)
— activities
— feedback on questions and activities
— informal style
— examples
— checklists
— job aids
— summary sections.

HOW TO GET THE LEARNING PACKAGE

We shall now look at the three ways of acquiring an open-learning package with the features you need. These are:

— buy a package off the shelf, adapting it as necessary

— write a study guide to resources which may not in themselves be in open-learning form (eg, textbooks; a practical kit)
— write your own package from scratch.

The first of these is much the quickest and cheapest route. It is outlined in Section Two (pp 18–30).

The study guide option, where you take existing materials which may not in themselves be in open-learning form, is not as quick or easy. But it is still likely to enable you to get your scheme running more quickly, cheaply and conveniently than if you had to produce your own package. Section Three takes you through the stages of designing and writing a study guide (pp 31–63).

The third option is sometimes necessary, for example when no suitable learning packages of any kind exist. This option is covered in other volumes in the Open Learning Guides series: Volume 2 shows an author how to write objectives, self-assessment questions and activities and Volume 6, *How to Communicate with the Learner*, discusses ways of structuring a package. *How to Communicate with the Learner* also discusses style, format and illustrations. Volume 7, *How to Manage the Production Process*, describes the process of production of a package from manuscript to finished copy.

WHY USE EXISTING MATERIALS?

In spite of the other options many schemes still go ahead and produce their own materials. In doing so they run into such problems as

— difficulty in recruiting good writers
— lengthy and expensive training for writers
— long delays in offering the scheme, while the package is put together
— stress, especially for project managers
— escalating expense
— waste of resources.

Why, then, do projects choose this difficult option? Firstly, schemes tend to drift into the position of writing their own material. Few providers commit time to carrying out a positive search for packages. This activity has to begin at an early stage of planning the course.

Secondly, teachers and trainers like to 'do their own thing'. Writing has a glamour about it, until the job begins. We are fond of reinventing the wheel.

Thirdly, scheme providers are not aware of the complexity involved in writing a package. The requisite skills do not always come easily; rarely is a good classroom teacher immediately able to translate his expertise into packaged form.

The arguments for choosing one of the other options are thus compelling. Time, money and effort should be saved. The end product is more likely to be good. The energies of teachers and trainers can be deployed in areas where they are more likely to bear fruit, for example in devising flexible support and management systems. Philip Waterhouse in *Managing the Learning Process* (see Booklist) sums up the situation: 'Making resources is so time-consuming that it can completely dominate the preparation phase. The results are often inadequately presented, poorly conceived, poorly designed, and unattractively reproduced. Use home production only when other sources have failed to produce what is required.'

Hence the current emphasis on using ready-prepared learning materials. This is the key to FlexiStudy, the open-learning system based in the further education sector. Colleges buy in learning materials produced mainly by the National Extension College and then tailor support and management systems to suit. Each contributes at its point of strength: NEC its expertise in package production, the colleges their experience in reaching, tutoring and supporting learners. NEC is ideally placed to make good packages but poorly placed to offer support to learners; the local FlexiStudy colleges are ideally placed to support learners but poorly equipped to write learning materials of sufficiently high quality.

Similar arrangements operate abroad, as can be seen in the extract below.

It was decided that the production of high quality courses by North Island College was beyond the finances available at that time, so a decision was made to buy in from the best sources available elsewhere and to concentrate on an efficient delivery system. Liaison was developed between the college and Athabasca University (then based at Edmonton, Alberta) which was loosely modelled on the Open University. This led to a co-operative arrangement and allowed a system called 'dual-student' status. This means that a student at North Island College can register for an Athabasca University course and is registered as both a university student and a college student. Athabasca University provides the course material and carries out the evaluation; North Island College provides the locally based student support system including promotion, advisory, tutoring, learning centre resources, library support, laboratory facilities, telecourse facilities, study space, group meetings etc. This has advantages for both institutions in that the university can spread its costs over a much larger student population and has much lower delivery costs, and the college has university level learning opportunities for students plus university accreditation.

Extract from 'New Learning Systems: some Canadian approaches', Coombe Lodge Report Vol 15 No 8, 1982, published by and reproduced by permission of the Coombe Lodge Further Education Staff College, Blagdon, Bristol BS18 6RG.

In this book we suggest that, while a package will never be exactly what you want, it is easy to adapt materials that are basically sound. Your learners can then benefit from someone else's package, adapted and personalized.

JOB AID: ROUTE TO SELECTING A PACKAGE

To summarize this section we include a job aid on pp 13–14 to help you to make decisions about the learning package for your scheme.

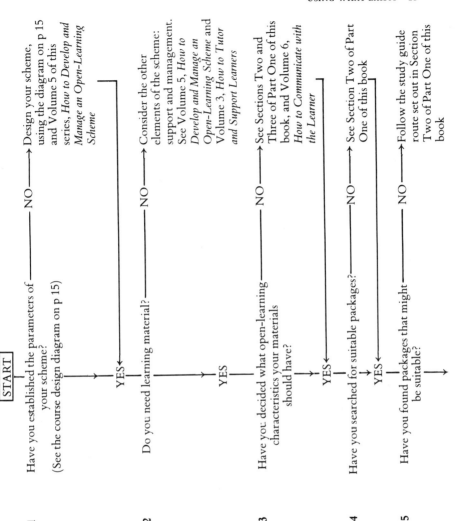

START

1 Have you established the parameters of your scheme? (See the course design diagram on p 15) — NO → Design your scheme, using the diagram on p 15 and Volume 5 of this series, *How to Develop and Manage an Open-Learning Scheme*

YES

2 Do you need learning material? — NO → Consider the other elements of the scheme: support and management. See Volume 5, *How to Develop and Manage an Open-Learning Scheme* and Volume 3, *How to Tutor and Support Learners*

YES

3 Have you decided what open-learning characteristics your materials should have? — NO → See Sections Two and Three of Part One of this book, and Volume 6, *How to Communicate with the Learner*

YES

4 Have you searched for suitable packages? — NO → See Section Two of Part One of this book

YES

5 Have you found packages that might be suitable? — NO → Follow the study guide route set out in Section Two of Part One of this book

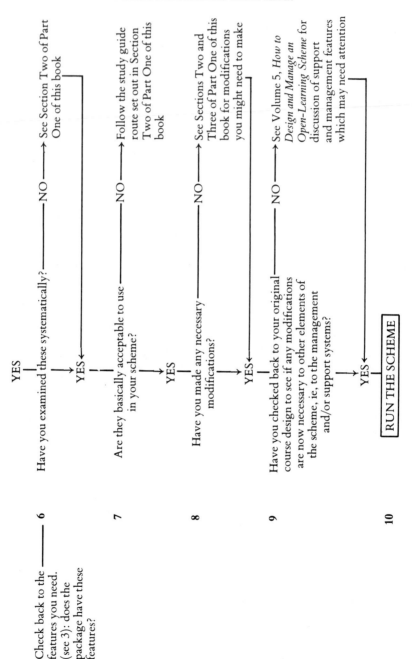

6 Check back to the features you need. (see 3): does the package have these features? — YES → Have you examined these systematically? —NO→ See Section Two of Part One of this book

YES ↓

7 Are they basically acceptable to use in your scheme? —NO→ Follow the study guide route set out in Section Two of Part One of this book

YES ↓

8 Have you made any necessary modifications? —NO→ See Sections Two and Three of Part One of this book for modifications you might need to make

YES ↓

9 Have you checked back to your original course design to see if any modifications are now necessary to other elements of the scheme, ie, to the management and/or support systems? —NO→ See Volume 5, *How to Design and Manage an Open-Learning Scheme* for discussion of support and management features which may need attention

YES ↓

10 RUN THE SCHEME

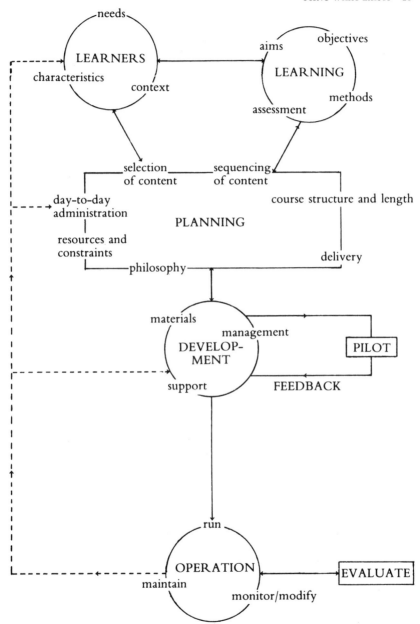

This diagram reminds you that selecting and adpating materials is only part of the total picture. It is explained more fully in Volume 5, *How to Develop and Manage an Open Learning Scheme.*

Q Quiz

1. Which of the following three statements is closest to the approach taken in this book?

(a) It is possible to decide whether or not a package is suitable for use in open learning by checking whether it meets a number of generally agreed criteria.

(b) Any materials might be suitable for use in open learning. Everything depends on the nature of the scheme and the learners in it.

(c) There is general agreement that packages for use in open learning should include features that support an individual as he works alone. But the precise features needed will differ from scheme to scheme.

2. This section suggests three routes to getting the right package for your scheme. List these in order, beginning with the easiest.

3. Why should a scheme try to avoid producing its own package from scratch? Can you think of two reasons?

Answers

1, (c). Schemes differ greatly — for example in objectives, content and learners, and in the degree of tutorial help provided. This variety makes it impossible to set out in advance *exactly* what the learning package should include. So (a) is not the best response. There is no one agreed set of criteria that defines an open-learning package, but there is general agreement that such packages should include supports to learning. These supports enable an individual to study productively on his own, probably for a substantial proportion of the course. (b) is thus a little too casual in its phrasing. (c) is therefore closest to the approach taken in this book.

2. Buy in a ready-made open-learning package. Use resources which may not in themselves be in open-learning form and prepare a study guide to them. Write your own package.

It is possible to think of exceptions to this order, but usually it holds good.

3. The following reasons are given or implied in this section of the book:

— it takes longer
— it costs more
— it requires skills many of which may be unfamiliar
— it is a complex process
— few institutions are set up for materials production

— it is stressful
— the end product may be poor
— training is necessary
— it diverts energy from other tasks
— it wastes resources
— it may be unnecessary as it duplicates what already exists.

Section Two. Finding, Evaluating and Adapting Open-Learning Packages

INTRODUCTION

This section is divided into three parts. The most substantial is the first part, which covers where and how to look for ready-made open-learning packages. Sources of such packages, or information about them, may be local, regional or national. The second part introduces a checklist which you can use to assess the suitability of the packages you find. 'How to adapt packages', the final part, raises issues of package modification which are taken further in the following section of this part of the book, 'Preparing a study guide'.

Objectives

After working through this section you should be able to carry out the following activities in your own scheme:

— search systematically for ready-made open-learning packages
— assess the usefulness of the open-learning packages you find
— list minor modifications which you may need to undertake.

WHERE AND HOW TO LOOK

Planning your search

Before you search you should have planned your course. You should have considered all aspects of design (see page 15). You will then know what kind of package you are looking for.

The following diagram sets out some of the main sources of information about packages. The sources are organized according to geographical location. The best starting point for you will depend on your circumstances.

If you are in industry you might look first at your company training resources, possibly located regionally.

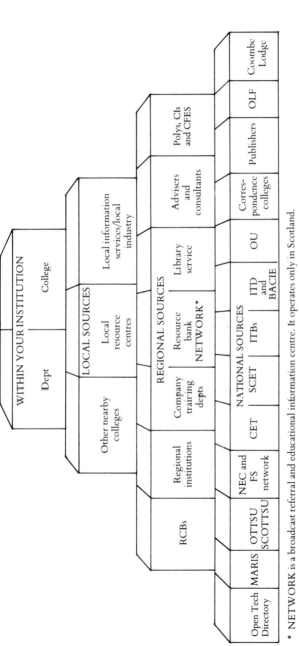

* NETWORK is a broadcast referral and educational information centre. It operates only in Scotland.

Key

BACIE	British Association for Commercial and Industrial Education	NEC	National Extension College
CET	Council for Educational Technology	OLF	Open Learning Federation
CIs	Central institutions (Scotland)	OTTSU	Open Tech Training and Support Unit
CFEs	Colleges of further education	OU	Open University
FS	FlexiStudy	Polys	Polytechnics
ITBs	Industrial training boards	RCBs	Regional curriculum bases
ITD	Institute of Training and Development	SCET	Scottish Council for Educational Technology
MARIS	Materials and Resources Information Service	SCOTTSU	Scottish Open Tech Training and Support Unit

If you are planning a FlexiStudy scheme you might contact a local college. Or, failing that, send for the list of FlexiStudy colleges published by the National Extension College, find one that offers courses you are interested in and then ring up the college coordinator.

If you need information about packages for technicians, managers or supervisors, then the Materials and Resources Information Service, MARIS (see p 21) should be your first port of call.

If you are running a workshop based in a college then your starting point might be the bookshelves and stock cupboards of your own institution.

> in 1976 my first priority was to attempt to collect together whatever individualized learning packages had already been produced commercially. The first place to look was in my own College, in locked cupboards. Some eight or nine years previously the College had set up an 'academic service unit' and had spent a fortune on programmed learning materials in many subject areas in book, filmstrip and cassette form. Transferring the relevant mathematical materials to the Workshop gave a reasonable start to its development.

Extract from 'The Bradford Mathematics Workshop' in 'Open Learning in Action: some case studies', Open Learning Guide 1, 1984, p 147, edited by Roger Lewis and published by the Council for Educational Technology

We give notes on each level of the pyramid on p 19, starting with what might be immediately available in your own institution and working through to national sources of information on materials.

Within your institution
Communication can be surprisingly bad within an institution, whether it be a company or a college. What you need may be nearer than you think. Somebody may have prepared a package already, even if it hasn't quite seen the light of day. Someone else may have carried out a materials search. Your librarian may know both about in-house materials and good learning packages that are commercially available. He may be prepared to carry out a search for you, if you give him time.

Publicize within your own institution what you are doing. This makes it more likely that you will discover what lies ready to hand. You might run a seminar and ask for support for your open-learning initiative. Or set up a committee to ensure that open-learning developments are coordinated. Or compile a register of relevant materials and experience within your institution. Such a register could include details of:
— course material in full open-learning format
— learning materials which include some self-study features
— handouts and other teaching materials which could be adapted
— other learning resources
— sources of information (eg, catalogues)
— expertise possessed by colleagues, eg, in the writing, design and layout of learning materials.

One further education college in Scotland discovered that a newly appointed lecturer had written several self-study packages in his previous job and had considerable expertise. But it took a staff development day to link the lecturer with the open-learning project.

Local sources
Local sources could include colleges, resource or information centres and any libraries, whether public or institutional. A local company may well have a resource person able to tap into national networks of materials, just as a local librarian or college librarian can offer services beyond the limits of his institution.

Sometimes the package you want may be available within a local institution but not on the open market. Release of such material is easier to negotiate locally than regionally or nationally. Deals can be struck — 'if you let us use your catering package we will let you use our computer literacy materials'.

Regional sources
Many regional resource banks have excellent communication systems, including online access to databases such as ERIC (Educational Resource Information Centre) or BLAISE (British Library Automated Information Service) which give details of book and non-book resources. They may also be aware of centres with specialist information in your own locality.

Some regions have a library service which specializes in non-book materials. Company training departments often have a wide range of contacts in the materials production field. There are also regional curriculum bases and advisory services which hold details of some learning resources.

National sources
Note: the addresses of all organizations mentioned in this section can be found in the Appendix (pp 131–133).

Materials and Resources Information Service (MARIS)
The first source for many readers of this Guide will be MARIS. MARIS stands for Materials and Resources Information Service. It was set up early in 1983 by the Open Tech Programme to provide information on open-learning materials in technician, supervisory and management training areas. MARIS provides two databases, one of open-learning materials and one of resources for open learning. Both are on viewdata, accessed via either a computer or a viewdata terminal. Once online to the materials database you can select packages by title, subject, content, target group, key skill, subject level, qualification, occupation, study time, media, author, cost. Here are examples of requests you might make:

medium	→	'I should like details of *audiotape-based packages*
occupation	→	for *site supervisors*'
occupation	→	'What is there for *electricians* who need *updating* ← level
skill	→	in *fault-finding techniques?*'
study time	→	'I need short packages, *no more than three hours*
subject	→	of study, on *industrial relations*'

Users without access to a terminal or users requiring long searches can ask MARIS for computer printouts to be sent to them through the post. When accessing the

```
                                        1000a
            Select by Subject

            nter Subject Descri
mechanical engineering                        .
. . . . . . . . . . . . . . . . . . . . . . . . . . . . . . . . . . . . . . . . .




Key O#  for Package Enquiry Menu
```

```
                                     50a
  Materials for selected Subject

There are 10 packages detailed for
the entered Subject
   MECHANICAL ENGINEERING

Do you wish to see list (Enter Y/N)  _




Key O#  for Package Enquiry Menu,
```

Materials for selected **Subject**

1 FLUID MECHANICS

2 MANUFACTURING TECHNOLOGY LEVEL II

3 FABRICATION,FORMING AND JOINING
   SKILLS (FYT 4)
4 MECHANICAL MAINTENANCE II (MODULE
   J21) VOL.1
5 MECHANICAL MAINTENANCE II (MODULE
   J21) VOLUME 2
6 MECHANICAL MAINTENANCE II (MODULE
   J21S)
7 HEAT lOSS CALCULATIONS:BASIC
   TRAINING (MH213)
8 INTERPRETING MECH.ENG.SERVICES
   DRAWINGS (MH210)

Key O# fr Package Enquiry Menu,
    N# for next page1

Title: HEAT LOSS CALCULATIONS:BASIC
       TRAINING (MH213)

Content: ENVIRONMENTAL TEMPERATURES &
         HEAT CALCULATIONS NEEDED TO
         MAINTAIN THEM,HEAT
         LOSS/U-VALUES CALCULATIONS

Target: MECHANICAL SERVICES TECHNICIANS

Skill: CALCULATIONS

Level: USE BY PRACTITIONER

Key O# for Package Enquiry Menu,
    No# for Page, 9# for list

Examples of four screens of MARIS viewdata information

resources database, you can select resources by subject, type (eg, consultant), media (eg, video) and various other fields.
Both materials searches and resource searches provide you with a contact name. Your next step might be to request an inspection copy from the supplier; to check whether anyone locally has a copy of the package; or to contact the resource for a brochure.
MARIS is complemented by the Open Tech Directory. This is a catalogue of all products and services funded by the Open Tech Programme and is published by the National Extension College from whom further details may be obtained.

The National Extension College (NEC)
NEC is a national producer of high-quality open-learning materials. It also offers a range of services to institutions running open-learning schemes. It is the home of one part of the MARIS operation.
NEC produces information on FlexiStudy, including a list of all FlexiStudy centres, together with details of the courses offered. Write to NEC and ask for any of the following:

— a publications catalogue (includes materials in the media of print, audiotape, videotape, floppy disc)
— a home learning catalogue (details of NEC's correspondence courses)
— the open-learning services leaflet (services NEC offers to organizations wishing to set up open-learning systems)
— information on MAIL (a software program to generate fast feedback to learners in open schemes)
— a FlexiStudy pack (information on FlexiStudy, including the list of centres referred to above and advice on how to set up a FlexiStudy scheme)
— the open-learning training workshop brochure.

All NEC publications can be sent to colleges or companies on approval.

The Council for Educational Technology (CET)
CET is the publisher of this series of Open Learning Guides. It has an Open Learning Unit at Southampton which is also the base of OTTSU, the Open Tech Training and Support Unit. Write to CET for

— a copy of *OLSNEWS*, a regular free newsletter on open learning (Southampton)
— details of CET's publications on open learning (either office)
— a copy of *CET News* (a newsletter on CET's activities) (London)
— details of OTTSU's services (Southampton)

The Scottish Council for Educational Technology (SCET)
SCET is the Scottish counterpart of CET. It is notable for its Open Learning Unit which runs workshops on open learning, produces a series of Open Learning Papers (most of which are free) and houses the other part of the MARIS operation: MARIS Scotland. SCET has an industrial liaison officer who acts as the link between company trainers and SCET's resources — which include catalogues of films, videos and software. The Unit also sells a number of key open-learning publications including the Open Learning Guides series in Scotland. Write to SCET for

— open-learning information and publications
— a free catalogue of industrial training films and videos
— a course list for industrial training.

The cover of the 'Open Tech Directory', pilot edition 1985, published by and reproduced by permission of the National Extension College

Scottish Open Tech Training Support Unit (SCOTTSU)
SCOTTSU is the Scottish equivalent of OTTSU. SCOTTSU provides advice, consultancy and training for institutions wishing to set up and run open-learning schemes in Scotland.

Industrial training boards (ITBs)
These produce training materials and have a very good knowledge of the materials available in their own industry. The head offices of the ITBs currently operating (1985) are given in the Appendix (pp 131–132). A fuller list of industrial training organizations is available from the Sector Training Branch, Room E621, MSC, Moorfoot, Sheffield, S1 4PQ.

British Association for Commercial and Industrial Education (BACIE) and Institute of Training and Development (ITD)
These are two national training organizations.

The British Association for Commercial and Industrial Education (16 Park Crescent, London, W1N 4AP) is a voluntary, non-political educational charity founded in 1919. It is concerned with all aspects of vocational education and training and provides a range of services including a major library and information unit; a wide range of publications and training events and a monthly journal, *Transition — from education through employment.*

The Institute of Training and Development (5 Baring Road, Beaconsfield, Bucks, HP9 2NA) is a professional body for trainers and provides information and qualification schemes — including correspondence courses — to support the trainer at every level.

Both BACIE and ITD make their services available to members. Write to the organizations for details of membership.

Correspondence colleges
Some correspondence colleges, such as Wolsey Hall and Rapid Results, have a policy of offering their materials for use in other open-learning schemes. The Council for the Accreditation of Correspondence Colleges keeps a list of all the colleges in the UK. Write direct to the individual colleges for details of their publications.

The Open University
Materials produced by the Open University are also available for purchase. All materials from the undergraduate programme and the Centre for Continuing Education can be purchased separately. The Open University has catalogues of what is available.

Publishers of open-learning materials
Certain publishers produce materials that are suitable for use directly in open-learning schemes. Notable amongst these are the 'Breakthrough' series published by Pan Books — Breakthrough languages and Breakthrough to Business. Write to the publishers listed in the Appendix for details.

The Open Learning Federation (OLF)
The Open Learning Federation is a grassroots organization for providers of open learning, mainly in the further education sector. For a modest membership charge

members receive a newsletter. This sometimes includes details of learning packages. The OLF regions also organize occasional workshops and conferences.

The Further Education Staff College
The Further Education Staff College at Coombe Lodge is a national source of courses, publications and information for the further education sector. It has produced some helpful publications on open learning, several of which are referred to in the Open Learning Guides. Coombe Lodge does not publish materials directly for learners, nor is it a source of information on learning packages. But it is listed here because of its influence in further education.

The Open Tech Unit (OTU)
The Open Tech Unit of the Manpower Services Commission works mainly through its projects such as MARIS, but it is also a producer of information and publications in its own right. It publishes *Open Tech News* (quarterly) and occasional papers on open learning.

The national providers discussed above are grouped in the table below.

Databases of open-learning materials (and other related services)	Notably MARIS
Information on materials and other services for open learning, including consultancy	NEC, CET, SCET
Information, etc, for users/ practitioners in open learning	OLF
Publishers of open-learning materials	NEC, some correspondence colleges, some publishers, the Open University
Information and other services, not with a specific open-learning focus and not specifically on materials	ITBs, BACIE, ITD
Other national agencies	Further Education Staff College, Open Tech Unit

The following two extracts from case studies in Volume 1, *Open Learning in Action,* show different approaches to searching for existing materials.

materials problem was not a major constraint: the learner could buy suitable packages from the fairly extensive range of materials published by the National Extension College, and from other providers such as Wolsey Hall. I felt that for bridging courses simple materials could be developed by the College to meet its internal or local needs.

Extract from 'Open Learning at Luton College of Higher Education' in 'Open Learning in Action: some case studies', Open Learning Guide 1, 1984, p 190, edited by Roger Lewis and published by the Council for Educational Technology

Using existing materials. In the early days before Tutor Teach I looked at all commercially produced materials available: books (either self-paced individualized learning packs or standard texts); workcards; students notes; audio-visual filmstrips and programmes; overhead projector material; prepared master banda sheets; television; video and radio programmes; equipment such as statistical kits and calculators; games; computer-assisted learning materials.

I quickly discovered that the audio-visual and filmstrip programmes were very expensive and outdated and that the software produced for the micros was dull and repetitive. This is changing: software is fast becoming available which will make the micro an absolute necessity in any open-learning scheme. I am, therefore, currently setting up a network of ten micros.

But in 1976 my first priority was to attempt to collect together whatever individualized learning packages had already been produced commercially.

The next step was to decide the topics the Workshop ought to be offering to support the mathematics elements in all the College courses. There were particular demands for material to cover topics in the TEC, BEC O- and A-level courses and for basic numeracy.

I traced, through what was the Association of Programmed Learning and Educational Technology Year Book, all the book companies and concerns who had been producing programmed learning packages. On writing to them, it soon became clear that the production of these packages had not been a viable commercial proposition and that they had stopped producing them. As I was convinced that this was the way forward I realized that I would have to prepare materials myself on the topic areas needed to fill the gaps in the published resources. I began with basic numeracy.

Extracts from 'The Bradford Mathematics Workshop' in 'Open Learning in Action: some case studies', Open Learning Guide 1, 1984, pp 147 and 150, edited by Roger Lewis and published by the Council for Educational Technology

HOW TO EVALUATE PACKAGES

This section assumes that you have got the package. You now want to see whether or not it meets your requirements. You should at this point consult the list of characteristics you drew up earlier (see page 10). These will be peculiar to you and to your context. You should be able to turn this into a simple checklist to use to work out whether or not the package will suit your learners.

Here is a simple checklist. It has been drawn up by a business studies lecturer who wants to set up an open-learning workshop in his college.

Is the content broken down into sessions of no longer than two hours' study time each?

Are case studies included?

Are activities included?

Is the style 'adult' enough for businessmen as well as for young students?

Is the material up to date, especially on legislation?

Is the material attractive?

Is the package multi-media or, at least, are references given to other available media, eg, video, CBT (computer-based training)?

Note that the individual compiling the list was prepared himself to provide other dimensions, such as objectives, self-assessment questions, photographs and company literature. So these items did not appear in his checklist.

You should draw up a checklist that accurately states your own requirements; it is unwise to use a general all-purpose checklist, though three examples are given on pp 105–110 to give you ideas.

You will probably want to include others in reviewing the material — for example:

— colleagues
— tutors
— subject specialists
— an open-learning specialist
— target learners.

You will need to allow several days to get the views of these people. Once again we repeat the importance of allocating time to the activities of finding and evaluating packages. In the end this will be time well spent.

Activity

Activity

Draw up a checklist for your own use.

Use the advice given above as a guide.

HOW TO ADAPT PACKAGES

You won't find a package that fills all your requirements. But the package must be basically acceptable. If tutors or trainers are involved they must be happy enough to use it. Otherwise their lack of confidence will be communicated to the learners, usually with disastrous results. (See Volume 3, *How to Tutor and Support Learners* Sections 2 and 3, for a fuller discussion of this and its staff development implications.)

You will almost certainly have to adapt the package in some way. Some of this could be handled by tutors, eg, when they meet learners at tutorials. More probably you will put the modifying material into permanent form and include it with the package itself. You might, for example, want to issue notes which

— update the package
— relate the package content more closely to your particular learners' contexts
— refer to the machinery and processes used within a particular organization
— produce extra or different assignments or activities
— refer to other resources you are using in your scheme
— modify the material to cover a different examination syllabus.

We discuss package adaptation more fully in the next section.

Providers sometimes ask about copyright. If you buy the packages for use in your scheme then you can do what you like with them, as long as you do not resell them or make copies. You can add whatever you like and use only those parts you want, ignoring others. If you do want multiple copies of a package you may be able to negotiate special prices or a licensing agreement.

You may want to go back to the producer of the materials and ask if they will adapt the package for you. They may do this if they feel that sufficient sales will result, or if you can offer them enough money to make it worthwhile. Examples of such adaptations are the NEC *30-Hour BASIC* course, which has been twice modifed in this way: firstly, for use in Ireland (one new replacement chapter was bound into the printed text) and, secondly, for use in Austin Rover's Open Tech scheme, where the text was adapted for presentation on computer. Such adaptations are subject to formal agreements being drawn up between the parties concerned. The end-product is good learning material adapted to serve specific needs — at much less cost than it would take to develop the material from scratch.

Activity

Decide what modifications you want to make to the package.

Then read the next section of this book.

Section Three. Preparing a Study Guide

CONTENTS
Introduction
What is a study guide?
Why write a study guide?
How to write a study guide
Job aid: the study guide route

INTRODUCTION
In the previous section we considered materials which are themselves in open-learning form. These may need adaptation but they will contain enough support elements to make them suitable for use in open learning. This section considers rather different materials, those not designed for open learning but which the organizer of an open-learning scheme may nevertheless want to use. We shall call these materials 'core resources'.

There is no clear cut-off point at which materials become or cease to become 'open-learning materials'. Rather there is a continuum.

1	2	3	4	5
structured —	structured —	textbook —	unstructured —	list of
open-	learning	(or	resource	resources,
learning	materials,	equivalent)	material,	eg,
course,	not designed	which has one	eg, case-	booklists,
with many	specifically	or two	studies,	select
aids to	for open	support	Jackdaw-	lists of
the ind-	learning,	features	type	films
ependent	but with	(eg,	wallets,	
learner	some support	chapter	collections	
	features	objectives;	of photos,	
		exercises)	videos	

In this section we are looking at the materials shown here to the right of the structured open-learning course, with particular emphasis on categories 2 and 3.

The main part of the section is a step-by-step account of how to write a study guide.

Objectives
After working through this section you should be able to

— define a 'study guide'

— decide whether preparing a study guide would be useful in your context
— write a study guide.

WHAT IS A STUDY GUIDE?

A study guide is a set of notes, more or less substantial, provided in the form of print or in some other medium. The study guide accompanies another resource, or resources. The course content, and one or two aids to learning, are contained in the resources, which may be in any medium. The study guide helps the learner to use the core resource(s). It will often include most of the aids to learning described on page 10 and in Volume 6, *How to Communicate with the Learner*.

The core resource is frequently a textbook. Many textbooks are excellent. They organize a great deal of content in a clear way, and more recent textbooks show an imaginative approach to layout and illustration. Their drawbacks are, however, seriously limiting in an open-learning context:

— they may be difficult to read
— the content may not be sequenced in an order that makes sense to the learner
— the structure may be too diffuse (see Volume 6, *How to Communicate with the Learner*, for a discussion of 'chunking' the material and providing alternative routes)
— the resource will probably be designed for all-purpose use, ie, not structured for a particular scheme
— there may be little or no interaction with the learner — questions and discussion, dialogue
— there may be no clear statement of learning outcomes
— there may be a lack of attention to learning strategies, particularly those needed for success in open learning
— there may be a lack of attention to motivation, stimulation, reassurance
— much may not be relevant, eg, the learner may only need Chapters 2, 4, 7 and 9
— they may need updating.

Some of these points are summarized by Norris Saunders (1966):

'. . . the textbook is weak in that it offers little opportunity for any mental activity except remembering. If there is an inference to be drawn, the author draws it, and if there is a significant relationship to be noted, the author points it out. There are no loose ends or incomplete analyses. The textbook is highly refined . . . but the author does the thinking. (Quoted in 'How to develop self-instructional teaching', Open University, p 151, 1979).

If you can find a textbook that does cover a substantial part of the course then you can put the missing learner-friendly elements into the study guide. If you find a number of resources in more than one medium the study guide can provide the necessary links. Thus the study guide

— supplies the supportive framework
— helps users to learn
— fills any gaps in the content.

The learner moves from the study guide into the other resources and then back into the study guide; as in the following example.

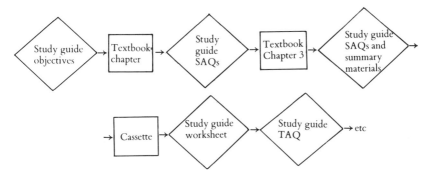

Key SAQ self-assessment question
       TAQ tutor-assessed question

In this example objectives and all assessment items are included in the study guide, together with summaries.

WHY WRITE A STUDY GUIDE?

The first reason is that you may not find a package that is itself in open-learning form. There are many more textbooks and other resources easily available on the market than there are open-learning packages.

Another reason is that to produce a study guide helps tutors and others in the scheme to feel they are fully involved. One of the problems of using purpose-made packages off the shelf is that tutors sometimes feel that they are losing a significant part of their job. If they are themselves responsible for part of the package they feel more committed and their conviction will rub off on the learners. Good teachers will, anyway, be already on the way to writing such guides. Existing handouts, worksheets and lesson notes will have some of the necessary features, for example:

— indications of what a group should be learning (aims and objectives)
— organization of the material in a user-friendly way
— grouping of work (eg, into lessons, half-terms, homework)
— examples
— definitions
— summaries
— assignments
— tips on how to approach assignments
— group activities
— advice on what to do if in difficulty
— questions and answers.

These are the characteristics of good teaching and some of these elements will be a familiar part of materials devised as an adjunct to conventional classes.

HOW TO WRITE A STUDY GUIDE

We now take you through a step-by-step approach to writing a study guide. We ought to preface it by saying that the art of writing study guides is in its infancy;

there is not a lot of experience to draw on.

Make sure that you have enough time for all the stages listed below, especially for stage 6, the pilot. This stage is the acid test, since it involves learners from your target group. If they don't learn from it, you've failed.

Summary of the stages

1. Draw up a specification for the whole package.
2. Choose core resources.
3. Decide what you have to put into the study guide.
4. Decide the format of the study guide.
5. Write the study guide.
6. Pilot the study guide.
7. Produce the study guide.
8. Monitor and revise the study guide.

1. Draw up your specification for the total package

You need to know, first, what the end-product will be like. What content will be included? What learning supports? What media will you use? You will need to refer to

— the objectives of the scheme
— the kinds of materials you think the target audience will be most likely to learn from
— the materials tutors/trainers will use productively (if using tutors).

You will need to think about the totality of the package: what the core resource(s) and the study guide will combine to produce. A careful analysis will help you to complete the next stage, which is to select the best available core resource(s). They will form the basis of your package. You will build your study guide around them. The resources may be

— a single textbook
— several textbooks
— an audiotape
— a videotape
— a computer-based training program
— a textbook plus audiotape
— a practical kit
— a computer-based training program plus videotape
— a practical kit, audiotape and set of worksheets
— any other combinations of the above elements.

Activity

Draw up a specification of what the total package will contain — ie, core resource(s) plus study guide.

Checklist

What content do you need?
What medium should the package be in?
What supports to learning should you include (see page 10)?

2. Choose core resource(s)

Before you write your study guide you will have to identify which core resource(s) you will need. We assume you have the various candidates to hand.

Here is one possible checklist of questions you may ask of each resource. Take note of how much you will have to put into your study guide to make each core resource suitable for use in your scheme.

1. Does it cover the right content?
2. Is the coverage extensive enough?
3. Is it up to date enough to be of use?
4. Is the structure flexible? Can it be reordered?
5. Is the level of difficulty right for the learners?
6. Will it be accepted by learners and their tutors?
7. Will it continue to be available?
8. Is it cheap enough?
9. Is the presentation attractive?

Here are some notes on these items.

1 and 2: it's better for the coverage to be too extensive rather than not extensive enough. You can always advise learners to ignore certain sections. But beware bulky resources, as these can be offputting (see items 6 and 9).

3: this will be of particular concern to your tutors or subject-matter experts and in areas where knowledge, skills, processes, etc, are rapidly changing. You can include a certain amount of up-to-date information in the study guide.

4: is it organized in a way that will help learners to use it and help you to write a study guide — eg, (if a book) does it have frequent headings, a clear contents page, sections of manageable length, an index?

5: if it's too difficult it will be unsuitable. Your study guide will not be able to carry the weight of constantly explaining the core resource(s). You can, though, deal with the occasional problem area.

6: this is a rather intangible item but you should be able to weigh up how acceptable the core resource will be in your own context. The learning package ought to have a coherent appearance. If the total package looks very fragmented or too diffuse it can put the learner off. Check whether you can repackage all the elements, perhaps putting them in a suitable box, folder or wallet.

7: this is surprisingly important. One of the drawbacks of using a core resource is that publishers can, without warning, allow it to go out of print. Or, less drastically, they may produce a new edition which makes all the references in your study guide out of date. You should write to publishers before committing yourself to a resource; the publisher should be able to tell you the likely inprint life. (If the resource goes out of print you may have to ask the publisher to allow you to reprint a stock for your own use.) This applies whatever the medium used for the core resource.

8: obviously important. Again, producers of learning materials can catch you out by sudden and dramatic price rises. You will know what you and the learners can afford. Give yourself some leeway.

9: you will know how attractive the package will need to be. For example, materials used in a workshop with a tutor constantly on hand can usually be less glossy than those which the learner has to study at home, alone.

You will have to consider how many core resources you will need. The more resources you choose:

— the higher the expense
— the more complex the study guide will be to write
— the greater the inconvenience to the learner

but

— you may not find just one resource adequate to meet the objectives of your scheme
— you may want learners to use several resources, for example, to weigh up different approaches to a topic.

You can sometimes compromise, for example, by finding the best available resource and producing a carefully selected, annotated booklist in addition to what you include in the study guide itself.

A course for a Scottish qualification made use of the text produced for a BTEC syllabus (*A Questions of Economics*) and added a routeing module to cover the syllabus changes. This took a fraction of the time required to produce an entirely separate package.

Activity
Choose your core resource(s).

3. Decide what you have to include in the study guide
You have now chosen your core resource(s). You next have to decide what elements are missing. These are the elements you will have to put in the study guide. Together, the core resource(s) and your study guide make up the total package.

Activity
Check back to your specification on page 34. List the items that are satisfactorily included in the core resource(s), and those that you must build into your study guide.

Checklist
Tick from the following list the elements you will need to add to your resource.

Explanation of the course; information on how to use the package.

Signposting between core resource(s) and study guide.

Purpose: aims/goals/objectives (see Volume 2, *How to Help Learners Assess Their Progress*).

Assessment/extra assessment (see Volume 2, *How to Help Learners Assess Their Progress*), for example:

— self-assessment
— tutor-assessment
— activities
— pre/post-test.

Feedback on assessment (see Volume 2, *How to Help Learners Assess Their Progress*).

Structuring aids (see Volume 6, *How to Communicate with the Learner*), for example:

— introduction, overview, etc
— routeing advice, signposting
— conclusions, review, summary.

Hints on how to approach the work, for example:

— study advice
— details of time likely to be needed for studying each section.

Additional content, for example:

— more examples
— material relevant to your learner's job, life, course, syllabus
— up-to-date information
— comments on the author's point of view
— contrasting viewpoints to the author's
— identification of key issues
— definitions
— explanation of concepts
— clarification of obscure points
— references to other reading/work
— indication of total time required
— any prerequisites before the learner can make use of the package.

You may want to add other things.

A note on chunking
One very important feature of the study guide will often be to break up the resource into manageable learning periods. Volume 6, *How to Communicate with the Learner*, discusses ways of doing this in a package constructed from scratch. Similar principles apply with a study guide. Each 'chunk' needs its own scaffolding, for example its own

— introduction
— objective
— list of items/equipment the learner will need
— content
— self-assessment questions and answers
— summary
— glossary
— assignment
— evaluation form.

Activity
Tick which of the above features you will need for each chunk. Add any others.

4. Decide the format of the study guide
You will be able to decide your format when you have finished stage 3. This will make it easier

— for *you*, to brief the writers of the study guide
— for *your writers*, who will know exactly what is expected of them
— for *your learners*, who will feel at home in a format which they can rely on.

One example of format is given opposite.

TASK ONE

Turn to Roger Lewis, How to Write Self-Study Materials.
Read pp 13-14, 'Characteristics of self-study materials'

This book is about print material but it has important
ramifications for multi-media provision.

Take each of the seven characteristics and give an example of
how you might use them from your own training perspective.

1. ....
   ....
   ....

2. ....
   ....
   ....

3. ....
   ....
   ....

4. ....
   ....
   ....

5. ....
   ....
   ....

6. ....
   ....
   ....

7. ....
   ....
   ....

(Do not spend any longer than 10 minutes on this)

I SUGGEST YOU DO NOT CONTINUE UNTIL YOU HAVE COMPLETED THE EXERCISES

Discussion

You will probably be aware now that for certain areas, some of these
characteristics are very difficult to achieve.

It is a challenge to talk about the mathematics formula in a lively
and interesting style, just as affective skills are difficult to
turn into clear objectives.

Roger Lewis lists the characteristics as:

1. What the learner needs to know	2. Providing objectives
3. Self-assessment questions	4. Study advice
5. Unpacking difficult concepts	6. Small segments of the subject
7. Friendly style	

Note that the style of the study guide can (should) be much more informal and
personal than that of the core resource. You are addressing your learners directly.

Activity
Decide the format of your study guide.

Write down the necessary details. These can form the basis of a briefing document for your authors, or a contract letter.

See Volume 6, *How to Communicate with the Learner,* for more help on the format of open-learning materials.

5. Write the study guide
Introduction
By now you should have

— decided what you want the total package to look like — ie, the core resource(s) plus your study guide
— chosen your core resource(s)
— decided what you have to include in the study guide
— planned your study guide format.

You are now ready to write the study guide. We shall work through an example. At stage 3 our imaginary course designer identified the following missing elements:

— user-friendly approach
— aims and objectives
— signposting and routeing
— assessment
— unpacking difficult material
— help sections
— summary and review sections.

These were not included in the core resource but since they were part of the package specification (stage 1), he wanted to include them in the study guide.

Activity
List the missing elements in your case.

As you read the following example decide how you will set about including the elements missing from the core resource(s) you have chosen.

Your elements will not be the same as those that follow, but the principles of operation will be the same.

User-friendly approach
You want the study guide to give a written equivalent to the friendly, supportive teacher or trainer.

Conventional class	Study guide equivalent feature
Now this next part of the course examines the main features of the banking system in the UK.	Aims and objectives
The set text by Foster and Preston makes the points clearly and concisely in Chapter 14.	
Could you turn to that chapter then (it starts on page 206). Read it quickly.	Signposting
Ignore the final page as it contains information we are going to cover next week. Now you will come across the concept of 'negative credit'. This means . . .	Routeing
	Unpacking
When you have finished that I want to have a brief discussion covering main points, then you can attempt these worksheet questions.	Summary and assessment
At the end of the class I'll give you a handout covering the main points.	Review
Any questions? . . . Good, if there are no problems, then turn to page 206 of Preston and Foster. You'll find it quite straightforward.	Anticipating problem areas
	Encouragement

The study guide replaces some of the commonest roles that the face-to-face tutor has to play. It should establish exactly the same kind of relationship to the textbook as the lecturer would: the textbook informs, but the lecturer guides and shapes.

Aims and objectives
Your study guide will usually break the resource into specific sections. Each section will have its own aims and objectives, defined in the study guide.

> This study guide covers a five-hour section of the course. When you have successfully worked through it, you will be able to
>
> (a)
> (b)
> (c)

You usually need to state objectives in your guide because your resources rarely include them. Or, if they do, they may not be relevant to your own course. Set your own objectives carefully, bearing in mind the learner's needs and the course structure. These should be aimed at the learner, and expressed in user-friendly language. The example overleaf comes from Nigel Paine at the Scottish Council for Educational Technology.

After working through this study guide and its related
material you should be able to:

1. Relate the role of materials to the open-learning
   system as a whole.

2. Pick out the main features of good self-study materials.

3. Write learning objectives to cover your own areas of
   interest.

4. Write a variety of self-assessment questions to test a
   trainee's grasp of course objectives.

You should complete the pre-course material in about 2½-4 hours.

Please have with you:

> This study guide
>
> (A Workbook on Writing Learning Objectives
>
> Enclosed   (How to Write SAQs
>
> (How to Write Self-Study Material
>
> Pen and notepaper.

THE INTRODUCTION AND CONTENTS PAGES ARE GIVEN OVERLEAF

CUSTOMER RELATIONS   21

UNIT OBJECTIVES
_____

Customer relations communication should create good
will between you and your customers. This unit shows
you how to do this with good new -- congratulations
and thank-yous -- and not-so-good news -- complaints,
adjustments, and collection notices.

INTRODUCTION
_____

Inquiry and response letters are part of the routine
of day-to-day business. Customer relations letters
deal with situations outside the normal routine.
Handling these potentially difficult situations
effectively is important to the success of any
organization.

Congratulations and thank-yous

Congratulations and thanks should be easy to offer,
because your audience is bound to be receptive...

Extract (below left) from the study guide that accompanies 'Mind Your Own Business', 1980, (p 21) published by and reproduced by permission of Seneca College, 1750 Finch Avenue, East Willowbank, Ontario, Canada

Signposting and routeing

Nothing is more annoying when you drive around a strange city than inadequate road signs. They lead you so far, then they appear to vanish. You drive round in circles looking for a hint of where you are and where you are going. A person familiar with the city will need only the occasional sign and will often find it difficult to recognize the problems faced by strangers. Everyone knows that you turn left at the crossroads — everyone that is apart from the stranger. Often an impression of a place is based on how easy it was to become familiar with it.

It is exactly the same when learning something new. It is unfamiliar ground to the learner, who can thus easily get lost and confused. For the author it is obvious; he can sometimes forget the need for clear route identification and the flagging-up of where the learner has got to.

Instead of	*You might put*
Read Chapter 6.	Read Foster and Preston, Chapter 6 (pp 110–125). There are five key points you need to look out for. These are: * … … … … … … … … * … … … … … … … … * … … … … … … … … * … … … … … … … … * … … … … … … … … Ignore the case study on the final page as we will be covering later the issues raised there.
Switch on the audiocassette and obey the instructions contained on it.	At this point switch on audiocassette number *two* side one. The cassette will give instructions on when to turn off and return to your worksheet. This cassette covers basic problems some engineers faced when turning to CAD (computer-aided design) techniques. It includes interviews with a number of engineers and a summary section which is repeated in the study guide on page 11. SWITCH ON THE CASSETTE NOW.
Now look at the main points again.	I have picked out the main points of this section as a self-assessment exercise. Please answer the six questions below. Then turn over the page to check your answers.

Assessment
In an open-learning package the individual should be able to chart his progress through the material. Self-assessment questions and activities are ways of helping him to see how far he is meeting the objectives. The writing of objectives, self-assessment questions and activities is covered very fully in Volume 2, *How to Help Learners Assess Their Progress.*

The same principles apply to assessment in a study guide. But you have, in addition, to lead the learner carefully from core resource to assessment section and back again.

You have now finished Chapter 6 of this book. Turn to the summary section in this Guide.

When you have worked through the summary section turn to the self-check questions on page 12. You will find responses and discussions on page 13.

If you are happy with your self-check exercise, go on to Section 3 which begins on page 14. This prepares you for your study of Chapter 9 of the book.

You can also use a tutor to assess certain objectives. If your course includes several core resources you can use tutor-marked questions to help the learner to pull these together and see the course as a whole. Advice on writing questions that a tutor will mark can be found in Volume 2, *How to Help Learners Assess Their Progress.* You can find an example of a tutor-assessed question on page 45.

Unpacking difficult material
At each stage you should ask yourself if you can make the learner's task more straightforward by your study guide. To do this you have to decide

— what the learners know
— what they might find difficult
— experiences your learners have which you can draw on
— which concepts need reinforcement
— how, in a conventional class, you would help a learner over difficulties
— how this can be converted into print or whatever other medium the study guide is in.

Ways of helping the learner master difficult sections include

— using worked examples, model answers, applied case-studies
— offering a glossary with the study guide
— putting difficult concepts into the margin, as in the medical example on p 45
— highlighting key sections
— giving an explanation of difficult points
— summarizing carefully
— clearly testing each part before asking the learner to move on.

The following three extracts are examples of different ways of unpacking a concept.

hypertension =
increased blood
pressure over a long
period of time,
maybe associated
with stress

Please turn to Chapter 4
of the textbook by Walker
and Goa. This discusses
the main causes of hyper-
tension amongst ethnic
minorities in Britain.
When you have finished,
attempt the self-check
questions over the page.

Extract from material by Nigel Paine

Ladies and Gentlemen!

Continuous Assignment

The Realworld Hardward Store

Part 14:   Expense Control and a BreakEven Chart

ASSIGNMENT FOR PART 14

(a) Using a budgeted income statement as the basis, prepare a list of the fixed expenses in one column and the variable expenses in a second column. Add the cost of goods sold to the variable expense total. Some expenses may be divided between fixed and variable.

(b) Using the column totals, prepare a breakeven chart for the hardware store on a grid. Assume that the store operated at 60 percent of capacity during the first year Below the chart indicate the sales volume is dollars and the percentage of capacity required at the breakeven point.

Extract from 'Outside help and inside risk', Unit 9, p 14–17, 'Mind Your Own Business',
1980, published by and reproduced by permission of Seneca College, 1750 Finch Avenue, East
Willowbank, Ontario, Canada

CLASS

In your answer to SAQs 1 and 2 you may have used the word 'class' and said that the two people (GP and shop assistant) come from different 'classes'. The word 'class' is very frequently used but often in a rather general way. We hear such statements as 'Britain is a class-ridden society' on the one hand and on the other, 'There's no such thing as class.'

SAQ 3: If I said 'The GP and the shop assistant come from two different social classes' what would you think I meant?

You may have written something like:

• they have different amounts of money;
• they have different life-styles;
• they have different chances in life;
• their parents were from different backgrounds;
• they have different amounts of importance and prestige.

'Class' can have a variety of meanings. This can make reasoned argument difficult, particularly in everyday contexts where people rarely stop to make clear the way in which they are using the word. Hence one of the first jobs of the social scientist, or indeed of anyone who wishes both to make himself clear and to understand others, is to define the terms he is using, in this case the word 'class'.

SAQ 4: Turn to your set book, Halsey.
1. Does Halsey use the word 'class'?
2. If so, where might we find a definition of how he is using the word?

This SAQ was deliberately phrased to make you think about your reading strategy. You need here to use a mixture of contents page and index – and common sense. The way to find out quickly whether or not Halsey uses the word 'class' is to look at the contents page and at the index. We're lucky first time – inspecting the 'Contents' shows up that Chapter 2 has the word in its title. We might thus expect a definition of 'class' either early on in that chapter or (just possibly) at the end of the previous chapter.

SAQ 5: Is the index any further help?

The index is not helpful – not, at any rate, in my edition; later editions may have a more comprehensive index. The index is in fact surprisingly unhelpful. On closer inspection you'll see that it contains only proper nouns – people's names, names of organisations (e.g. Trades Union Congress) or acts of parliament. You can thus find a reference to the Tridentine Mass but not to class and that's slightly peculiar, to say the least, in a book about social science. More useful indexes include concepts, like 'class' and 'status', as well as proper names.

As we predicted, Halsey offers definitions at the beginning of Chapter 2 – in the first five pages (in my edition pages 20-24 inclusive). Now it's important to say once again that Halsey's writing is far from easy to understand and the difficulty is likely to be most acute to someone who hasn't read much social science before. So don't be too alarmed if you find the following SAQ hard going. Be prepared to spend some time on it, say about 30 minutes.

Extract from 'Preparing for Social Science', 1981, p 59, by Roger Lewis and Liz Maynard, published by and reproduced by permission of the National Extension College

The authors then ask learners to underline phrases which suggest how the author of the core resource is using the word 'class'. This leads to a working definition of the word and further examples, to ensure that the learner understands, and can apply, this definition.

See also the section on 'How to encourage active learning' in Volume 6, *How to Communicate with the Learner.*

'Help' sections

Parts of the course may be extremely difficult for certain learners. These may include

— technical areas
— materials from a previous course, which the learner may not have covered
— statistical analysis
— using mathematical formulae
— interpreting graphs
— complex concepts or ideas.

You can use an optional 'help' section for these. The learner in difficulty can be routed into a section which deals more slowly with the difficult area and which includes further examples, self-assessment questions and other aids. 'Help' sections can be built into the study guide, offered as a separate printed item, or put into a different medium such as audiotape.

Learners not needing this kind of reinforcement are directed over the section, on to the next part of the course. A 'help' section thus loops away from the main thrust of the course.

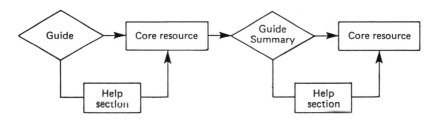

Your own judgement from teaching, together with evidence from piloting (see page 50), will indicate when a 'help' section is necessary.

Volume 6, *How to Communicate with the Learner*, has an extensive discussion of how to create different routes for learners according to their skills, purposes and learning styles.

Summary and review sections

An important role for a study guide is usually to provide regular summary and review sections. These

— pull together the main points from the core resource(s)
— form a basis for discussion and comment
— act as revision sections
— help to shape the material for the learner.

Summary/review sections can be in the form of narrative or set out as a checklist. Or you could devise a post-test section where the learner builds up his own summary section by responding to questions.

Summary sections do not simply come at the end of the study guide; they help to define each major section, though you could also reprint section summaries at the end of the guide. This then becomes a useful aid to revision. Overleaf are two alternative methods of reviewing the study guide section of this Open Learning Guide.

WHY A STUDY GUIDE?

To link disparate material.
To add an interactive, individualized and self-pacing format to core resources.
To fill gaps.
To select from other materials what is appropriate for your course.
To save time and money.

THE FEATURES OF A STUDY GUIDE

A user-friendly tone.
Overall course aims and objectives.
Sections.
Signposting.
Routeing.
Assessment questions.
Activities.
Feedback.
Assignments.
Unpacking difficult concepts.
'Help' sections.
Additional content material.
Summary/review sections.

Method 1. Checklist of points made

Please answer the following questions.

DO NOT LOOK AT THE ANSWERS UNTIL YOU HAVE COMPLETED THE EXERCISE

Your correct answers will form a convenient summary section.

1. WHY A STUDY GUIDE?

Tick which four *key* roles a study guide can fulfil:

(a) Linking disparate material ☐

(b) Covering all the course content ☐

(c) Enhancing core resources by adding interactive learning features ☐

(d) Putting forward a view which balances the author's point of view ☐

(e) Selecting what is appropriate from a core resource ☐

(f) Replacing notes taken by the learner ☐

2. THE FEATURES OF A STUDY GUIDE

Fill in the blenks from the word list below.

(a) The learner needs to know what he will achieve by the end of a course or a section of a course, so a study guide will contain ....

(b) To help the learner check for himself if the objectives have been achieved a study guide will contain ....

(c) The higher level objectives such as synthesis or evaluation can be tested by
. . . .

> *Wordlist*
> User-friendly tone
> Signposting
> Aims and objectives
> Summary and review
> Tutor assessed questions (TAQs)
> Self-assessment questions (SAQs)

Sample answers to the two questions

WHY A STUDY GUIDE?

The four *key* roles I noted were:

(a) linking disparate material; the study guide becomes the main point of entry and source of direction for the learners

(c) interactive learning features; the study guide has an important role in adding interactive elements to the core resource

(d) balance; if a core resource takes an 'extreme' position the study guide can add balance or at least alert the learner to the particular stance being struck

(e) selecting from the core resource; the study guide author will want to highlight certain parts of a core resource and either ignore or play down others

(b) and (f) are not areas a study guide should try to cover.

THE FEATURES OF A STUDY GUIDE

(a) The missing words are 'aims and objectives'. 'Summary and review' also have a role in this but they come at the end. The question asks what alerts the learner at the *beginning* of the course.

(b) The missing words are 'self-assessment questions (SAQs)'. SAQs check each objective. 'Summary and review' could be right if, for example, they include revision questions. 'Assignments' is not correct since these require a tutor; (b) refers to the learner checking *for himself.*

(c) The missing words are 'tutor-assessed questions (TAQs)'. These tend to test higher level objectives, though it is not their sole role.

Method 2. Post-test questions, the answers to which form a summary of the main points covered

6. Pilot

Whatever other short cuts you may take, you should not cut the stage of piloting. This is when you use a draft of your study guide with sample learners, note their reactions and then revise as necessary. Volume 6, *How to Manage the Production Process,* discusses drafting and piloting in detail and you should consult that book for a fuller consideration of the following summary (items before the third draft are pre-pilot):

— the first draft is checked by the author against a checklist (such as that on page 59)
— the draft is revised accordingly
— the second draft is shown to colleagues whose views are collected
— the draft is revised accordingly
— the third draft is clearly typed and tried out on a small group of learners from the target group.

The author watches them as they use the guide. He collects feedback. This is usually called 'developmental testing'. Then

— the draft is revised accordingly
— ideally the fourth draft is then tried out 'for real' on a larger group of learners, say 30–50 ('field testing' or 'validation')
— the draft is revised if necessary and then put through production.

Thus several cycles of drafting and revision are usually necessary to get a good end-product. Trying out the draft with some target learners, and getting their honest opinions, is probably the most important stage of all. Careful scheduling and management of time are vital.

7. Produce the study guide

Give thought to the look of the finished product. You want learners to use the study guide to the full. They are more likely to do this if it is well presented. Your study guide should, if possible, have all the qualities of well produced learning material, including illustrations and an attractive layout. It should not be overshadowed by the other components of the package.

Presentation issues are discussed in the companion Guides, Volume 6, *How to Communicate with the Learner,* and Volume 7, *How to Manage the Production Process.*

The importance of the study guide should also be stressed at every point in the scheme, for example in tutorial contacts.

8. Monitor and revise the study guide

You should check the performance of your study guide. You might do this by including an evaluation sheet (one is reproduced on pp 52–54) and by other methods such as talking to learners and tutors. Every so often you will need to update and modify your study guide in the light of the comments you collect and the performance of the learners.

A note on copyright

Copyright is only a problem if you want to reproduce information from other sources in your study guide. You will in this case have to ask permission of the copyright holder, normally a publisher. To do this you write to the copyright holder giving details of the source (title, author, publication date, a precise description of the extract you want to use, what you plan to do with the material (eg, who will use it, whether users will pay, the number of copies you intend to produce). These details will help the copyright holder to decide whether or not to charge you, and how much. You would be well advised to write early for such permission. It can take some time for copyright holders to reply and you sometimes have to negotiate.

Note that you do not need copyright permission if you or your learners are buying the source itself, ie, you are not yourself making copies of it. But copying even one small diagram taken from a publication will need copyright clearance. The exception to this rule is a publication called *Non-Copyright Graphics*. This includes drawings and diagrams which you can freely reproduce in your own materials without breaking copyright agreements (see the illustration on pp 55–56).

Pages 57–58 show a suggested form of letter to send when seeking copyright permission.

You could consult the following CET publications by Geoff Crabb for more information on copyright:
Copyright Clearance: a practical guide (Guidelines 2), 2nd ed, 1981
Information sheet no. 6, 'Copyright'
Copyright Agreements Between Employers and Staff in Education.

For advice on particularly difficult problems, write to or telephone the Rights Development Officer at CET, 3 Devonshire Street, London W1N 2BA (01–636 4186).

DISTANCE LEARNING
DISTANCE LEARNING
DISTANCE LEARNING
DISTANCE LEARNING
DISTANCE LEARNING
DISTANCE LEARNING
DISTANCE LEARNING
DISTANCE LEARNING
DISTANCE LEARNING
DISTANCE LEARNING
DISTANCE LEARNING
DISTANCE LEARNING
DISTANCE LEARNING

CNAA Postgraduate Diploma in Educational Technology

STUDY UNIT AND ASSIGNMENT EVALUATION FORM

Please return this form with your Assignment submission

1. Student's name .... Intake .... Date ....

2. Title of Course Assignment ....

3. How long did you spend on:
   the study units relevant to this assignment? ....
   the assignment itself? ....

4. Please note any parts which seemed to take you an excessively long time.

5. How long after the last relevant study unit did you do this assignment?

6. Did you find the teaching materials sufficiently related to the assignment requirements?

7. List any words, ideas etc. that were not explained clearly enough or that were assumed incorrectly to have been known already (NB. Please give name of unit).

DUNDEE COLLEGE OF EDUCATION

8.   List any objectives you feel you did not achieve.

9.   Did you do any follow-up work or additional study before you completed the assignment? Please give details.

10.   In what ways did you find the teaching materials relevant to your job needs?

11.   In what ways did you find the assignment materials relevant to your job needs?

12.   Did you do the activities? (YES/NO)
      If so, was this useful preparation for the assignment?

13.   Did you do the post tests? (YES/NO)
      If so, was this useful preparation for the assignment?

2

14. Did you find that the stated criteria for marking this assignment gave you sufficient guidance on what is expected?

15. Were there any parts of the assignment requirements which were unclear or difficult to understand?

16. Please give any other comment on individual units, or the assignment eg. in terms of length; degree of difficulty; interest value etc.

FORWARD PLANNING

Please indicate your own personal deadline for your next assignment submission.

Title of Assignment:

Target Date:

Thank you for your help.
Please return this form with your assignment submission.

GM/ST
10/84

3

'Study Unit and Evaluation Form' for the CNAA Postgraduate Diploma in Educational Technology, published by and reproduced by permission of Dundee College of Education

Examples of graphics for copying supplied by Graphics World Ltd

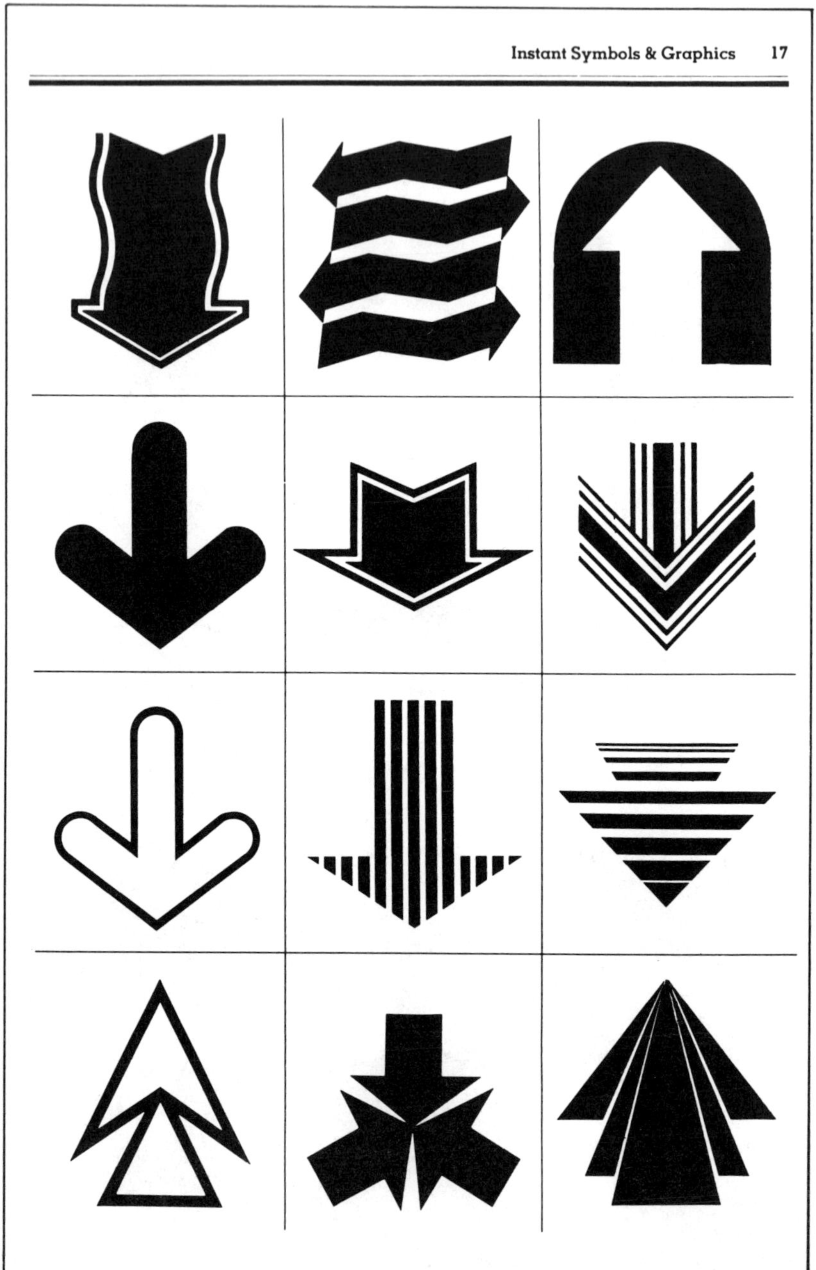
Instant Symbols & Graphics 17

Council for Educational Technology

3 Devonshire Street, London W1N 2BA *Telephone* : 01-580 7553/01-636 4186 *PRESTEL* : ✳ 211 ⧣
Chairman : Professor J C West, CBE *Director* : G Hubbard

Open Learning Guides Project
Coordinator:

Please reply to:

Tel:

Dear

Request for permission to reproduce copyright material

Would you please confirm that, as the owner of the reproduction
rights, you are agreeable to the Council reproducing the material
listed overleaf for the purposes stated. Full acknowledgement
of the source will be made. If you are not authorised to grant
these rights, would you please let me know who I should contact.

To save you time and trouble, the return of this letter or a
photocopy of it, duly authorised in the space provided would be
sufficient.

Yours

COUNCIL FOR EDUCATIONAL TECHNOLOGY FOR THE UNITED KINGDOM

Description of material

Reproduction required for

A series of open learning guides to be published by the
Council for Educational Technology in 1984 and 1985.

I/We, as owners of the reproduction rights, agree that the
Council may reproduce the material for the purposes stated.
We require no fee/We require a fee of ..... for these rights.
(Delete whichever is inappropriate)

Date .... Signed ....

Note: fees are payable if and when the right granted is
exercised.

Letter sent to copyright owners of material used in this book

C

Checklist
Summary checklist for writing a study guide

1. Have you drawn up a specification for the whole package?

2. Have you chosen your core resource(s)?

3. Have you decided what material/open-learning features will have
to go into the study guide?

4. Have you decided the format of your study guide?

5. Have you drafted your study guide?

6. Have you cleared copyright as necessary?

7. Have you piloted your study guide?

8. Have you produced the study guide in an attractive form?

9. Have you set up arrangements to monitor, update and revise the
study guide?

A Activity
Check your end product against the following checklist.

C Checklist
Are the necessary open-learning features included?

Is the study guide material well ordered?

Is the study guide written to a consistent format?

Is signposting between core resource(s) and study guide clear?

If several resources are used are they well integrated?

Is cross-referencing kept to a minimum?

Are references to the core resource(s) exactly pinpointed (eg, not just by chapter but by page; not just by page but by the opening and closing words)?

Is essential work distinguished from optional?

Is the guide likely to interest the users?

Is the guide well produced and attractively presented?

JOB AID: STUDY GUIDE ROUTE

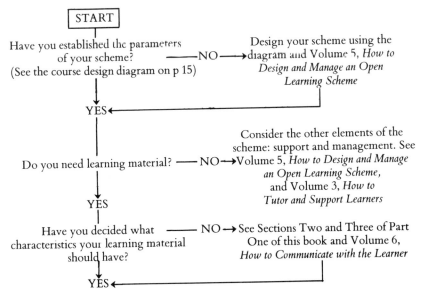

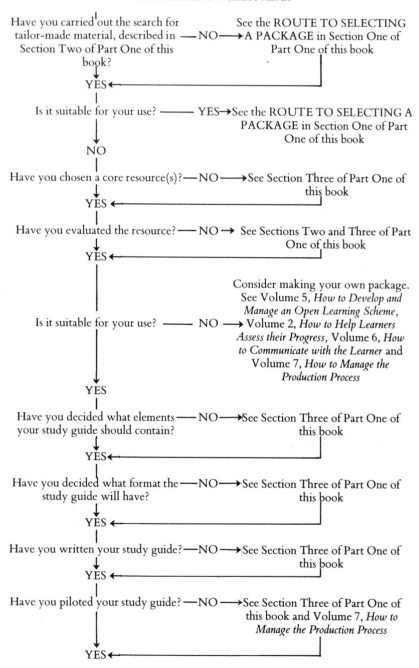

Have you carried out the search for tailor-made material, described in —NO——➤ See the ROUTE TO SELECTING A PACKAGE in Section One of Part One of this book? Section Two of Part One of this book?

YES ◄

Is it suitable for your use? ——— YES➔See the ROUTE TO SELECTING A PACKAGE in Section One of Part One of this book

NO

Have you chosen a core resource(s)?—NO——➤See Section Three of Part One of this book

YES ◄

Have you evaluated the resource? —NO ➔ See Sections Two and Three of Part One of this book

YES ◄

Is it suitable for your use? ——— NO —➤ Consider making your own package. See Volume 5, *How to Develop and Manage an Open Learning Scheme*, Volume 2, *How to Help Learners Assess their Progress*, Volume 6, *How to Communicate with the Learner* and Volume 7, *How to Manage the Production Process*

YES

Have you decided what elements—— NO ——➤See Section Three of Part One of this book your study guide should contain?

YES ◄

Have you decided what format the—NO——➤See Section Three of Part One of this book study guide will have?

YES ◄

Have you written your study guide?—NO ——➤See Section Three of Part One of this book

YES ◄

Have you piloted your study guide? —NO ——➤See Section Three of Part One of this book and Volume 7, *How to Manage the Production Process*

YES ◄

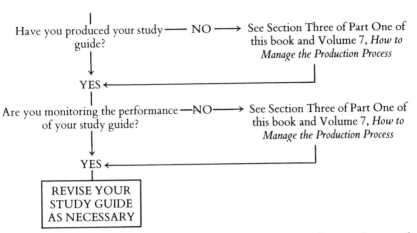

Have you produced your study —— NO ——→ See Section Three of Part One of
guide?   this book and Volume 7, *How to*
                                         Manage the Production Process

YES ←

Are you monitoring the performance —NO——→ See Section Three of Part One of
of your study guide?   this book and Volume 7, *How to*
                                         Manage the Production Process

YES ←

REVISE YOUR
STUDY GUIDE
AS NECESSARY

Two of the case-studies in Volume 1, *Open Learning in Action,* make extensive use of study guides. Relevant extracts are given below.

> We also use existing print materials such as textbooks and journal articles but we always provide study guides with self-assessment questions.

Extract from 'The YMCA Distance-Learning Scheme' in 'Open Learning in Action: some case studies', Open Learning Guide 1, 1984, p 209, edited by Roger Lewis and published by the Council for Educational Technology

> In Tutor Teach the programme of work for a student taking a complete maths course is based on a set textbook. The textbook is accompanied by study guides called 'units'. Each unit consists of a booklet on a topic or group of topics and contains instructions for the student to read specified parts of the textbook and work through specified exercises. Comments are provided on points of difficulty. Topics not in the textbooks are fully explained, and mistakes or misprints are corrected.

Extract from 'The Bradford Mathematics Workshop', in 'Open Learning in Action: some case studies', Open Learning Guide 1, 1984, p 150, edited by Roger Lewis and published by the Council for Educational Technology

Quiz

1. Which of the following definitions of 'study guide' is nearest to that used in this section?

(a) A booklet, or equivalent in another medium, which gives advice on study skills, for example, how to draw graphs, how to write a report.

(b) A booklet or equivalent in another medium, which helps the learner in an open-learning scheme to study productively from one or more resources not themselves in full open-learning form.

(c) A booklet explaining the administrative details of the course — eg, when to contact a tutor, the qualifications that may be gained, dates by which assignments must be submitted.

2. This section suggested eight steps to writing a study guide. These are printed below, out of sequence. Place them in the recommended order.

Choose core resource(s)
Decide the format
Pilot the study guide
Monitor the study guide
Draw up your specification for the total package
Produce the study guide
Write the study guide
Decide what the study guide should include

3. Two lists are printed below. The left-hand list is of some of the stages in the process of producing a study guide. The right-hand list gives reasons for these stages. Match items in two lists, eg, if you think the reason for piloting is to help your writers to prepare the study guide manuscript then you will match (c) with (ii).

(a) Draw up your specification for the total package	(i) See what target learners think of your study guide
(b) Decide the format for the study guide	(ii) Helps your writers to prepare the study guide manuscript
(c) Pilot	(iii) Helps you choose the most suitable core resource(s)

4. The aims and objectives in your study guide may vary from those in the core resource(s). Tick which of the following reasons may explain this. (You may tick more than one.)

(a) The core resource(s) may have aims and objectives which are far broader than the ones suitable for your course.
(b) The aims and objectives of the core resource(s) may be in a language which is not easily understood by your learners.

(c) The core resource(s) may include too many aims and objectives.
(d) The core resource(s) may not include any aims and objectives.

Answers

1. (b) is the closest definition.
Here are comments on the other two options.
(a) A study guide could well include advice on how to study, but it will include other things as well.
(c) Again, this could be part of a study guide but as it stands the definition is not inclusive enough. (c) is more likely to be in a course handbook; such a publication is described in Volume 6, *How to Communicate with the Learner.*

2. Draw up your specification for the total package
Choose core resource(s)
Decide what the study guide should include
Decide the format
Write the study guide
Pilot the study guide
Produce the study guide
Monitor the study guide

The above order is suggested in this section. You may choose to tackle the steps in a different order, to miss some out, or to add others of your own.

3. (a) and (iii)
(b) and (ii)
(c) and (i)

There are other possibilities, eg, (c) and (ii) (in a sense you could argue that any of (a), (b) and (c) apply to (ii). Here are some comments on our pairings.

(a) and (iii). If you know what you want the package to do in your scheme you are more likely to choose suitable core resources.
(b) and (ii). If your writers know exactly what features to include, and when and how to include them, they will find it easier to prepare manuscript.
(c) and (i). The purpose of piloting is to get feedback on the study guide from the people whom you were intending to help by producing it.

4. Any of these could be the reason, ie, you could tick any or all of them.

Part Two. How to Select Media

Introduction to Part Two

In the first part we looked in some detail at how to obtain open-learning materials, how to adapt them and at how to build packages from what already exists. In the second part we are more concerned with the principles which you can use to guide your selection and use of media. This part therefore follows on from Part One but will also be useful for the person producing open-learning materials from scratch and wishing to consider a range of potential media.

The first section defines some principles of media selection. We then give a summary of the advantages and disadvantages of various media and of how you might use them in open learning. We do *not* set out to cover any of the technical details, for example how to use a video camera. We assume that you will either subcontract such work, or hand it to an in-house expert. You will need to brief people extremely carefully, so we cover the educational and training background to media choice. We assume that you are managing an open-learning project, acting as an author, or taking part in a planning team.

Each section of this part of the book has an introduction which includes a statement of objectives.

Section One. How to Select Media

CONTENTS
Introduction
Cautions
Principles for selecting media

INTRODUCTION
In this book we deal with the medium or media chosen for the package itself, not the media for support. (You will find a discussion of media for support in Volume 3, *How to Tutor and Support Learners.*) The boundary is not, however, always a clear one. The telephone can, for example, be used both for support and for the transmission of course content.

In this section we begin with some words of caution before outlining some principles that could guide your selection and use of media.

Objectives

After working through this section you should be able to

— define what we are covering in this book when we use the words 'medium'/'media'
— avoid common misconceptions about media choice
— follow sound principles when selecting media.

CAUTIONS
Some very common errors are made when choosing media. Here are those most frequently encountered by the authors of this book.

(1) The medium for the learning package is chosen too early in a project. Or not even 'chosen' — people don't give it any serious thought; they just assume it will have to be presented in print, on videotape or (more commonly these days) as a piece of computer-based training material.

(2) The medium is chosen for the wrong reasons — eg, 'the boss likes it', 'it's the in-thing', 'we've got all the necessary facilities'; 'it's the medium of the future'; 'we bought the hardware last month so we might as well use it'. The only good reason for choosing a medium is because it is appropriate to the learners and the context in which they work.

(3) It is assumed that high technology media are inherently more powerful or more exciting than low technology media. This is an insidious misconception. It ignores the importance of choosing an *appropriate* medium. It also suggests that the technology itself is a guarantee of good learning material. This can never be so; only

good course design can create a sound learning package. It is also worth bearing in mind that the more complex the medium the more difficult it is to realize its potential.

(4) It is assumed that the correct medium can be arrived at by a scientific process of choice. This is the reverse of 1, 2 and 3 above; instead of no choice, or a lopsided/wrong-headed choice, the course designer overdoes it and spends too long trying to select media scientifically. There is in fact no scientific way of selecting a medium. A medium's potential, and the ultimate impact you achieve, depend on a large number of variables such as experience of working with a particular medium, professional support, the time available for development, etc. The point is reinforced by the following quotations.

'No one has yet developed a coherent theory of educational media which will determine that, for a particular educational task, one medium should always be used rather than another,' *Big Medium, Little Medium,* W Schramm.

'The idea of a multi-media slot is very attractive; put an educational problem into the slot, and out at the bottom comes a recipe showing which medium is best for solving it. Unfortunately, no one has yet built one. Each medium has strengths and weaknesses, but these are not so clear, or so different, that we can say things like "Always use television for teaching art" or "Radio is no good for mathematics" or "Print is no good for people who cannot read or write". (There is, for example, evidence *against* each of these three statements.) The research that has been done is, in fact, inconclusive. Most of it suggests that any medium can be used effectively for almost any subject, if the students are well motivated and the circumstances favourable,' Unit 2, 'Choosing what media to use', *Administration of distance teaching institutions,* International Extension College, p 17.

Experience shows that:

— any medium *can* be an effective teaching tool
— practicalities usually govern the choice of medium (not for example, 'what medium is ideal for showing this topic?' but 'which media will the learners have access to?')
— common sense is the only scientific approach needed; the good course designer will weigh up a number of factors including characteristics of a medium, the learner's context, the objectives of the package, tutors' preferences and cost
— the way in which a particular medium is used is what matters.

These conclusions lead us to some principles we suggest you bear in mind when choosing between media.

Relate media selection to course design

Choice of medium is only a *part* of the course design process. It should be looked at in association with all the other relevant issues such as the objectives of the course, how learners will be assessed, the learning methods to be used. These issues are discussed in Volume 5, *How to Develop and Manage an Open Learning Scheme;* the master diagram from that volume is reprinted on page 15 of this book.

Consider your target learners carefully

This rarely happens when a medium is chosen. There are several aspects you need to consider.

Firstly, access: the farthest most schemes get is to assume 'Of course they'll all have access to videorecorders' or 'Ownership of computers in that social class is high'. Rarely are such statements properly checked. This is astonishing when you consider the implications of wrong choices — the cost and the time involved, particularly in developing media at the higher end of the technology range.

Secondly, how target learners are likely to react to the various media: the preferences, expectations, age-group and attitudes of your target audience are extremely important. Even if learners have access to a particular medium they may resist its use for educational purposes. Open University students, for example, didn't always use radio and television productively because they didn't consider them to be serious learning resources, and the fixed broadcast times were often extremely inconvenient for busy adults.

Carry out some market research on however modest a scale. Talk to some of your target learners about such things as how they like to learn, when and where they will study, how portable they would like the package to be.

If your scheme makes use of tutors/trainers you also need to consider them. Will they work productively with the medium you choose? Will they need any special training? Remember that the human being in a system, particularly if influential in the learners' eyes, can easily frustrate your plans.

Think about how you will use each medium

The particular medium you choose is less important than the use you make of it. Any one medium is capable of varied use. Just think of the following aspects of print (admittedly, one of the most flexible).

Format	*Approach*
A magazine	Words only
A learned journal	Words and pictures
A newspaper	Serrated for tearing off
A popular paperback book	Sticky-backed
A glossy brochure	Full of blank space for
A technical manual	people to write things in
An architect's drawing	
Playing cards	
Separate sheets	
Sheets bound together	
Sheets in a ring binder	
Different sized sheets in a wallet	

The article by Duchastel (1982) mentioned in the Booklist has further ideas.

Consider using more than one medium

It is often a good idea to use several media for the package, rather than just one. People differ in their preferred ways of learning things; some, for example, like to learn from print, others to use their ears.

A change of medium can also be stimulating. Courses in the Henley distance learning programme, for example, encourage the learner to turn from print to videotape and then to audiotape. But see the next principle.

Integrate media

Integration can mean different things, depending on your reasons for using several media. You may, for example, be transmitting much the same message in two or three different ways. Purists consider this bad practice but the same message communicated in different ways can be justified on the grounds mentioned above, ie, learners can then choose their own preferred point of access. Repetition can also mean reinforcement. If you are using different media in this way then the job of integration is relatively easy, though you should always try and see the package as a whole and make explicit links between elements.

You may be using media more ambitiously, for example deliberately using each medium at its point of strength. This route was chosen by the Open University. This form of integration means giving much thought to what each individual medium achieves best. For example: television — case-studies; print — concepts; audio — talking through complex diagrams; kits — practical experience.

Bates describes one successful example of this kind of integration. In M101 (a maths foundation course) the media were linked much more closely than is usually the case. Essential material was incorporated only in the television programmes; students would seriously prejudice their chances if they missed them.

If you use several media you will probably want to use one as the 'anchor' medium. This will usually be print. Your anchor medium will guide the learner to use the other media. It will act as the link between say audio, video and a computer package.

Use the simplest medium possible

Some schemes admit to the phenomenon of 'media drop down', ie, starting with a complex medium and ending with a simpler. 'Media drop down' occurs usually through learner pressure. The Dundee College of Education Diploma of Educational Technology scheme is an example. The benefits of working in a variety of media did not overcome what learners considered the inconvenience and 'fiddling' involved in, for example, moving from print to filmstrip and audiocassette. The learners felt print's portability an important factor. The course team in the end agreed to turn some filmstrip/cassette programmes into print only.

Remember also that a plethora of media can be very offputting to a learner: it can all seem too much to handle.

The only other media used are audiocassettes and filmstrips, both of which must be returned by the student. The cassettes carry personal introductions to set the scene and examples, but more use could be made of dialogue and discussion. Filmstrips contain frames of photographs, artwork or captions and they may be used in conjunction with the sound track. We find that students prefer the main input in text form. They are happy to use cassettes or filmstrips when they are essential to the communication, but many find it tedious to have to use any equipment at all, even a cassette player.

Extract from 'Educational Technology at a Distance from Dundee College of Education' in 'Open Learning in Action: some case studies', Open Learning Guide 1, 1984, p 175, edited by Roger Lewis and published by the Council for Educational Technology

Use media that are easy to control

Where possible go for a medium over which control is easy. This mainly applies to learner control. Learners are more likely to use the package if they feel in control of it. But the degree of control course writers and tutors can exert is also important. Writers are likely to feel a greater commitment to preparing material for a medium they understand, use and can themselves shape. Audiotape is an example of a medium which can, if necessary, be managed entirely by the writer, without the need for the intervention of 'experts'.

If tutors are to be expected to use the medium — eg, on their own in working through the course or in meetings with learners — it is wise to consider their skills and preferences. If, for example, they don't bother to watch television programmes this is likely to reinforce the same behaviour in the learners.

Remember: the more complex the media, the greater the likelihood of technical problems. Such problems are extremely irritating to learners, for example a computer program which shows up error messages with no further explanation.

Use each medium interactively

If the package is to be used in open learning it will need the features discussed in Part One of this book and, more fully, in Volume 6, *How to Communicate with the Learner*. These features include

— a clear statement of objectives
— self-assessment questions, activities, assignments and feedback
— the ability to get an overview, for example of content, of assignments, of the kinds of self-assessment questions
— the ability to use the package flexibly, for example by skipping or by choosing a variety of sequences
— the convenience of being able to stop studying and resume easily at the right place
— adequate signposting
— unpacking of difficult concepts
— help sections
— regular summaries and reviews
— a friendly tone and conversational style.

Packages in the newer media often lack these features. They should be capable of at least the same degree of flexibility as print. (See 'Information technology using open learning: interactivity analogue', by Paine for a detailed example.)

Exploit the media for your package for your support system

Link the package (whatever medium it is in) to your learner support system. Ann Jones (see Booklist) gives an interesting example of this. Open University students, working at computer terminals in study centres, were in touch at the same time electronically with a tutor. If they needed help they could contact this tutor; conversely, the tutor could observe what they were doing and himself intervene. The students liked the facility of voice contact with their tutor and appreciated the link with a person, even if they didn't actually need to use it. Thus the learners could move between the package and the support system in an unusually flexible way.

Take particular care when choosing new media

There are several reasons for this rather unfashionable statement. The following considerations are drawn from an excellent treatment of the topic written by Tony Bates. (See the concluding essay in *The Role of Training in Distance Education.*)

Criteria for use in open learning

In most open-learning contexts media must be cheap, reliable, easy to use and multi-functional. Several of the newer technologies do not as yet meet all these criteria. Interactive video programmes, for example, are usually costly to design and software developed for one system may not be compatible with other systems.

Ownership of equipment

Much open-learning is carried out at home. The statistics of ownership of hardware, projected forward to 1990, are not encouraging for those who favour newer media. Bates gives the following estimates.

	Percentage of householders owning relevant hardware
Broadcast radio and television	98
Audiocassette	90
Telephone	80
Videocassette	66
Microcomputer	50
Cable television	40
Viewdata	30
Teletext	20
Videodisc	10

1990 Projection of ownership

Before choosing a medium you have to be very sure that your target learners will have the relevant hardware. One Open Tech project is planning to use video, audio, computer and PRESTEL. Its learners will need: a BBC Model B microcomputer, a videorecorder, an audiocassette recorder, a modem, a PRESTEL licence and a printer. Even with discounts the cost of this equipment (before the cost of the course is added) is over £1000 (1985 prices).

Bates reckons that if 80 per cent or more of your target learners own, or will buy, the relevant hardware you can reasonably use that medium. Less than 50 per cent ownership either means you cannot consider using a medium or you will have to provide learners with the necessary equipment. The real problem is in the 50–80 per cent category. This includes microcomputers, where there is the additional problem of lack of compatability, ie, your learners may own a computer but it may not be compatible with the system you plan to use.

If learning takes place in a centre other than the home it can often be easier to use newer media. But funding for hardware is not always available and equipment may not be owned by the appropriate department. This may also prevent some learners from taking the course if they cannot come to the centre.

Media limitations

Some of the newer media are inherently limited in their potential for use in education and training; for example, teletext. See the next section of this book.

TECHNOLOGY	EXAMPLE	REACTION
'NEW' TECHNOLOGY	Computers PRESTEL	Exciting Happy boss Good press
COMPLEX EQUIPMENT	Tapes, kits, video	Looks good Could go wrong
CHEAP MEDIA, RELIABLE, EASY TO USE	Print	Oh, not that

Based on a diagram by Richard Freeman, Executive Director of the National Extension College

Technical expertise

The more sophisticated the medium the greater the complexity of designing the package. The solitary course writer, or small team, will be unlikely to possess the skills necessary to develop a high technology package.

This creates a potentially dangerous split between on the one hand staff with professionalism in learning, close to the target users, and on the other the programme producers. One answer is to set up a team. But who should lead the team? What professional boundaries will have to be overcome? The larger the team the more difficult it is to manage, the higher the cost and the longer it takes to produce anything.

Bates points out: 'the real danger is that the subject expert will be further distanced from the students through having to work through intermediary producers or "transformers", who will impose their own standards and requirements over the teaching materials. For the use of technology in distance education to become really widespread, the technology has to become so simple that ordinary teachers and students can use it with minimal training.' 'Putting it together: now and the future' in *The Role of Technology in Distance Education*, p 226.)

On the other hand, training materials using new technologies in-plant can actually help overcome 'distance' from the materials providers by offering such things as online support.

 Quiz

1. This section sets out principles according to which we suggest you can choose the medium for your scheme. Tick the *three* statements which are closest to principles stated earlier.

(a) Choose the simplest medium which will do the job.

(b) Since tutors and learners are conservative about media, you have largely to disregard their views.

(c) High technology media are more effective than low technology media.

(d) The medium you choose is less important than how you use it.

(e) Choosing your media is part of the course design process.

(f) You can choose your media by applying scientific principles.

Answer

1. (a), (d) and (e) are three of the principles we suggest. Here are some comments on the other alternatives.

(b) Tutors and learners *are* often conservative, but you would be unwise to ignore their views. The package is designed for learners' use and unsympathetic tutors can wreck all your good intentions (though to some extent training can overcome conservative attitudes).

(c) As it stands this is untrue. High technology media may be very powerful but in certain circumstances they can be less effective than low technology media. Everything depends on who the learners are, where and what they are studying and on the other related matters discussed in Volume 5, *How to Develop and Manage an Open Learning Scheme*.

(f) We argue that there are no known scientific rules or formulae for deducing the 'correct' medium to use in any particular case. You can only use the skills of good course design.

Section Two. The Media

CONTENTS

INTRODUCTION

In this section we consider — in note form — the advantages and disadvantages of various media for use in open learning, from the points of view of learner, designer and producer. Awareness of the limitations and potential of each medium, together with knowledge of your course and learners, will allow you to make sensible choices. Inevitably we are unable to go into detail, and to qualify all the points we make, so we refer you frequently to further sources of reading and information.

Objectives

After working through this section you should be able to

— decide which media may be worth considering for a particular task
— use the job aid in Part Three to choose media for the package in your scheme.

PRINT

Points for

Portable.

No equipment required.

78

Permanent record.

Familiar to learners.

Easy to use in a range of ways (eg, intensively; skimming; skipping).

Relatively cheap both to generate print-based material and to reproduce it.

Distribution is relatively straightforward.

Easy to update in certain forms (eg, looseleaf/ring binder).

Many packages are available to choose from.

Easy to modify text using a wordprocessor.

Print can be used extremely flexibly.

Points against
Requires a literate audience.

Can be too familiar, unexciting and thus ignored. (Too much like school?)

On its own not particularly effective for objectives involving feelings and skills.

Linear.

Hard to conceal answers.

Storage and distribution can be a problem in certain circumstances (but see the quotation below).

Hard to update, eg, if bound as a book.

Full-colour printing is expensive.

Uses
Very good as an anchor/linking medium.

Print's portability and ease of use are particularly important in open learning.

Good for topics with a high 'non-moving' content.

Learner can personalize and modify by writing on it.

Can incorporate photographs and diagrams.

Examples
These are too numerous to list.

As far as the authors are aware, every open-learning scheme uses print in some way.

See the case-studies in Volume 1, *Open Learning in Action*. Print forms a significant part of all of them except possibly 'Sight and Sound'.

Notes
See page 71 for the diversity of print.

Imaginative use of print can overcome linearity.

Microfiche can be used as a medium for distributing print.

In many distance-learning institutions I have visited around the world they have an impossible burden of stock on the shelf which it is uneconomic to update. At Peterborough we have installed a Xerox 9400 which can reduce if necessary and produce 120 prints a minute on both sides of the paper, delivering them in collated sets. This is marginally more expensive than offset litho, but it means that, when appropriate, the run length can be just the number that is required for immediate use, leaving one master on the shelf for easy updating.

Extract from 'Open Learning at Peterborough Technical College' in 'Open Learning in Action: some case studies', Open Learning Guide 1, p 242, edited by Roger Lewis and published by the Council for Educational Technology

SLIDES AND PHOTOGRAPHS
Points for
Little or no equipment needed.

Easy to use.

Portable.

Can be used in conjunction with another medium, eg, when listening to audiotape or reading print-based unit.

Distribution straightforward.

Gives good visual detail.

Can brighten up a package.

Points against
Duplication can be awkward.

Difficult to arrange/rearrange the sequence.

Special packaging sometimes required.

Uses
Excellent for details of equipment or processes not needing movement.

Reinforcement of print-based content.

Can be used for case study analysis.

Packages with scientific or technical content.

Examples
See Dundee College of Education case-study in Volume 1, *Open Learning in Action*.

Medical packages make use of slides.

University of Guelph Agricultural Extension packages make extensive use of slides in filmstrip format.

Notes
Items must be clearly labelled or it is not obvious when they should be used.

AUDIOTAPE

Points for
Easy, quick and cheap to produce.

Familiar, widespread technology, equipment cheap and robust.

Easy to store.

Cheap to distribute.

Easy to update (since usually cheap to remake tape).

Unthreatening, personal, intimate.

High degree of author control possible; no complex production process.

High degree of learner control, convenient.

Can be recorded on by learner and returned to tutor.

Points against
Can be difficult to find relevant part of tape.

Complex branching/routeing is difficult.

Requires access to a player, restricts portability.

Requires concentration; some content, eg, a logical argument, may be hard to follow.

Uses
To provide human contact, advice.

To talk learners through the contents of a learning package.

To get updating/errata messages/extra help to learners.

Sounds, music, discussion, case-studies and debate.

Feedback on interpersonal skills.

For language pronunciation work.

Examples
British Institute of Innkeepers Open Tech project uses audiotape for

— helping learners through difficult textual material
— stimulation, eg, of group discussion
— encouragement.

BBC (and other) language courses — practice of oral skills.

'On the line', Open University telephone tuition and counselling training package uses audiotape:

— to present case-study material
— to lead into role plays
— to demonstrate ways of using the telephone
— to humanize the print component.

Notes

Note the advantages of combining with print — two media, both easy for learner to control, easy to make, cheap, familiar and portable.

Cf broadcast radio: audio is more flexible, more convenient; cheaper; less formal, easier to prepare and integrate into a package.

Costs

Durbridge (see Booklist) quotes £300 and £3000 range to make a tape in the OU, including academic and clerical time, BBC studio overheads and copying (1984 prices).

Distribution

Durbridge quotes 50p from master tape to delivery to student. One hour of tape could provide 2–3 hours of student learning, ie, 25p or less per learning hour once the master tape has been prepared.

Portability

Tapes are ideal for use in car; new portable machines make it possible to use whilst walking, or travelling by train.

Support

Same technology can be used for communication of support (eg, from a tutor) as well as for the package (see Volume 3, *How to Tutor and Support Learners*).

SLIDE/TAPE

Points for

Relatively easy to produce and edit/update (eg, replace a slide, re-record a tape).

Relatively cheap to copy.

Very good for colour.

Continuous playing possible.

Uses two channels of communication.

Visuals can be varied (photographs, diagrams, graphs, cartoons). So can sound (voice, music, sound effects).

Plenty of slide/tape programmes are available.

Can be transferred to video.

Points against

Tedious to load/set up.

Can seem slow or clumsy unless expensive equipment used.

Branching is hard to build in.

Cannot show movement.

Ready-made slide/tape programmes are often expensive to buy (£20–£300, 1984 prices).

Uses
For talking through a complex diagram/manual skills.

To introduce variety on a low budget.

Where colour quality is important (eg, art appreciation).

Examples
Slide/tape is widely used in industrial training but is not much used in open learning. The Dundee Dip Ed Tech course uses filmstrip and sound, but comments that students on the course sometimes find it irritating to have to set up the equipment.

Notes
This mixture of media is variously called 'tape/slide', 'slide/tape', 'sound/slide', 'audiovision'. The tape is usually cassette but it could be reel-to-reel; filmstrip or microfiche can be used instead of slides.

Filmstrip is easy to send through the post; hand-held viewers are so cheap they can be given to learners. Filmstrip and small viewers also make the medium more portable, though learners may complain that they are 'fiddly'.

Necessary to jusitfy slides rather than, say, printing the visuals in the text.

Slide/tape can now be used in random-access or computer-controlled modes (see below).

Random-access slide/tape machines
It is now possible to buy a kit which allows slides to be selected at random from a normal carousel. If this is linked with a computer program it allows a high level of interactivity between the learner and the slide/tape programme (or slide/computer program). This does minimize some of the disadvantages listed above but it obviously increases costs dramatically.

It is now possible to buy a random-access cassette tape machine which has exciting possibilities for interactive learning. This too can be linked to a computer to select segments of the tape depending on learner performance or learner choice.

There are therefore a number of different forms of slides/tape packages. These are shown below, moving from the simplest to the most complex format.

Slides supplied with an audiocassette, not physically or electronically linked.

Linear slide/tape programmes including pulsed tapes for automatic slide selection.

Random-access slide/tape machines.

Interactive (and computer controlled) slide/tape.

Straightforward

Complex

VIDEO

Points for

Many video programmes exist and could be used as part of an open-learning package.

Can be attractive to some learners.

Familiar to some learners.

Uses two senses — sound and sight.

Can show movement. (Normal speed, slowed down, speeded up.)

Realism — illustrates complex situations.

Directness.

Points against

Learners sometimes expect high standards of finish — this adds to expense.

Costly to make (from £100—£1000 per minute of finished film) 1984 prices.

Equipment not portable.

Formats can be incompatible: tapes recorded on one system will not play on another.

Learners approach with 'TV' expectations rather than an active learning orientation; hence danger of passivity.

Can date more easily than print.

Uses

Demonstrations, eg, of complex skills/continuous processes.

For dramatic effect.

When the real world is too

— big
— small
— fast
— slow
— inaccurate
— dangerous
— invisible
— distant.

Simulations

Examples

The AnCO Marketing course and other upmarket business courses, eg, from the OU and Henley Management College.

Note

This is the first medium so far considered that can show movement.

Two contrasting views of video

> We rejected videotape right at the beginning as being too expensive as a distance-learning medium, though we do use video and film at residential courses. Colour illustrations are not necessary since we do not have to introduce new objects or places to our students. We have found that carefully used print and audiotape can help the student to achieve affective and skills acquisition objectives. He can be encouraged to use the real world as a laboratory. Our support system can then develop this process.

Extract from 'The YMCA Distance-Learning Scheme' in 'Open Learning in Action: some case studies', Open Learning Guide 1, 1984, p 212, edited by Roger Lewis and published by the Council for Educational Technology

Henley Open Management Education reported, 'We felt we had to include on video more than two hours of material, divided into study sessions and fully integrated with all other materials, containing a dramatised case study, interviews with operating managers, discussions with experts and the use of a simple model to illustrate concepts.'

COMPUTER-BASED LEARNING

Points for

High potential for interaction with the learner.

Sequencing, etc, can be adapted according to

— learner's existing knowledge
— rate at which learner works
— learner's style.

Provides immediate feedback.

Can provide random generation of test examples.

Can conceal/withhold answers and responses.

Good at branching.

Very easy to update/amend.

Standards can be guaranteed — standardized training.

Enables the learner to study in privacy.

Some learners like the medium, eg, its novelty value for learners turned off by formal education.

The hardware can often be used for a wide range of purposes.

Hardware can easily be added, eg, a printer for hard copy.

Points against

Can be very expensive to design software that exploits advantages of the medium to the full.

Expertise required — development of courseware often needs a team.

Limited sound and graphics on many machines.

Some learners dislike the medium.

Some machines and software are unfriendly to the user (whether author or learner).

Access — where will learners use the computer?

Are sufficient machines available and are they in the right places?

Not easily portable.

Incompatibility problems, eg, software may run only on particular machines.

Health hazards associated with VDUs.

Equipment can be expensive.

Uses
Excellent for keyboard training and simulation.

To motivate certain groups, eg, young adults (novelty value), managers (privacy).

Probably greatest use is to manage learning, eg, to route the learner around a multi-media package; to test learning readiness; to maintain learner records; to provide evaluative data on the learning package (eg, how long learners took over a particular question). But these management facilities are rarely used.

Simulations; to apply theory to a practical model, eg, running the British economy.

Examples
BBC Computer Literacy project (described in Volume 1, *Open Learning in Action*).

Several schemes financed under the Open Tech Programme are using computers as a presentation medium (eg, HCITB; Austin-Rover; ICI).

See Dean and Whitlock in the Booklist.

Notes
Called by various names, eg, 'computer-based training', 'computer-based learning'. The computer may be used to display learning material and/or to manage learning (CML).

Beware the tendency to confuse what the computer can theoretically do with what in practice normally happens. Time and other resources (especially skills) are needed to exploit the full potential of the computer. These resources are rarely available and the computer is then used as an expensive and inefficient page-turner, with few of the interactive features necessary for open learning.

Use of 'author' languages to create CBT materials can cut costs but reduce authors' freedom to incorporate exactly what they want.

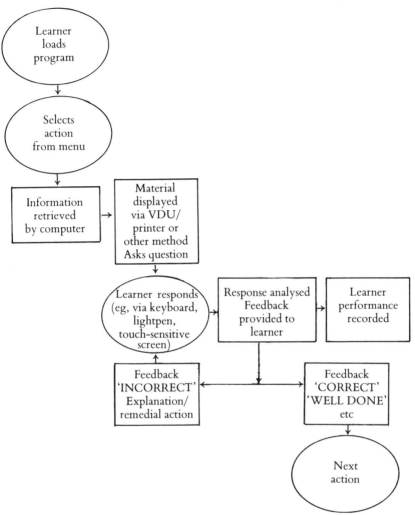

Typical cycle for computer-based training or interactive learning material, based on a diagram in 'Management Training Series XA 615 Computer Aided Training', published by and reproduced by permission of the Construction Industry Training Board

INTERACTIVE VIDEO

Introduction

Interactive video is a term used to describe the linking of video and computer technology — basically a computer (or microcomputer) and a video source (tape or disc) plus a television set (or monitor). Information from either computer or video can appear on the screen in the form of graphics, text, motion or still pictures. The term 'interactive' refers to the way in which the learner's response influences which sections of the package are presented next — for example, the learner is asked a question and his response is interpreted by the computer, which selects a relevant sequence. Thus material can be presented in any order and branching is easy. An even more 'open' use of interactive video is to allow the learner to explore a database, and to initiate his own learning process, without waiting for prompting or questions (see the two quotations on p 90).

Interactive video may involve a videodisc or videotape: if a disc, approximately 54,000 frames are separately and randomly accessible on one side. Videodisc is more sophisticated than videotape but is more expensive to produce. It is impossible, at the moment, to update a videodisc. The difference between disc and tape are discussed by Parsloe (see Booklist).

Types of interactive video

Disc-tape player with onboard microprocessor.   Limited

Tape player linked to simple external control.

Tape player linked to microcomputer.

Disc player linked to microcomputer.

Fully integrated workstation and/or simulator.   Complex

Points for

Very flexible — (1) on disc, two sound tracks can contain different material, cover different levels of difficulty or be in different languages; (2) the driving software can be modified. The same video material can thus be used on a variety of courses.

Integrates the advantages of previously separate technologies, especially computer and video.

(When well programmed) offers a remarkable degree of adaptability to the individual, very interactive.

Can provide:

— live action (cf. film/video)
— dramatization
— simulation
— voice over moving footage (original soundtrack replaced by commentary)
— voice over stills (eg, photographs/artwork)
— captions, eg, names of people, places and things
— text — with or without sound
— split screen — half or quarter or any; separate material on each part.

Link to computer offers built-in learning management (see previous section on computers).

Uniformity: same material always presented, complete and accurate.

All tape or disc contents are under learner's control.

Videodisc can store text, still pictures, software or graphics.

Points against
Can be costly and time-consuming; production usually requires a team of specialists and even these need to master new technologies, eg, more complex video production techniques.

Access to hardware needed.

It is easy to confuse what is theoretically possible with what is usually the case.

Uses
Powerful encyclopedic capacity — vast amounts of information can be stored on one disc and be randomly accessed.

Each disc equals a library. The whole of the *Encyclopedia Britannica* could be stored on one side of a videodisc.

Powerful simulations can be presented.

Safer and less expensive than conventional training for certain occupations (pilots, doctors) (cf. training of underground train drivers).

Examples
At the time of writing few interactive video programs are generally available; the technology is developing rapidly and much experimentation is taking place.

One example given (in *CET NEWS 18*, June 1983) is a videodisc on repairing a bicycle. With all its parts labelled the learner points to the part he wants to learn about, say the gear. A sequence on the workings of the gear immediately appears. This includes a moving sequence showing how the gear works. The learner can view this at a variety of speeds, or frame-by-frame. If he wishes he can select a sequence on maintenance including the tools required and a branching programme on how to use them. At a touch on the screen the learner can move in and out of any of these sequences.

Several interactive video packages are currently (March 1985) in development with part-funding from the Manpower Services Commission and Department of Trade and Industry.

Open University 'Teddy bears' videodisc.

Online storage and retrieval (training materials for library staff).

Notes
In view of costs, it is very important to carry out a feasibility study before committing resources, and to build in a pilot once the project goes ahead.

You must be able to justify use of interactive video, for example:

— you must be able to afford it
— there should be sufficient numbers of learners to justify the investment
— learners should have regular access to the relevant machines to run the system.

Selection of system
Disc-based.

Tape-based (eg, CAVIS).

Tape-based do-it-yourself (VCR + micro + low-cost interface).

Each has its own cost implications (contact MARIS: see Appendix).

Courseware
You may be able to adapt commercial courseware, soon likely to become available.

Learner reactions
Not much work has been carried out on how learners react to, and use, interactive video, but see Laurillard in the Booklist.

A note on costs from a reader, Dr Keith Roach

Interactive video is not *necessarily* costly, even in absolute terms. A colleague at the Polytechnic of Wales is successfully using interactive videocassette in routine teaching (10 workstations) — in-house produced, on lowband U-matic. The video production techniques are certainly not more complex, either. In fact, it is often the case that production techniques are simpler than in 'narrative' video, as it is a matter of a collection of separate, discrete segments, rather than of continuity, with mixes, fades, etc.

Two views of the use of interactive video

'If interactive video were to become as highly controlling and directive as most CAL has been, it would be a gross misuse of the medium, partly because it diminishes the potential variations in the use of stored data, and partly because it undermines the students' own responsibility for their learning. Giving the balance of control to the student has not only the benefit of being more democratic, it is probably also more educationally effective.' (Laurillard, D M, 'Interactive-video and the control of learning', IET papers on Broadcasting 231, published in *Educational Technology 236*, pp 7–15, 1984.

'I agree that interactive video is maximally exploited when used in such a learner-controlled fashion, but would argue against the suggestion that it should *only* be used in this way and in this context. It is undoubtedly very effective indeed when used in a rote-learning or drill-and-practice mode, being able to hold attention and interest for very long periods (at a recent professional exhibition, two groups worked right through a 90-minute IV programme of ours, with crowds pressing around them all the time!) and to correct errors very effectively — and in a way that the learner would not accept from a human tutor, very often. What degree of responsibility for learning has the student in a lecture, or a pupil in a class, or a trainee when being instructed on the factory floor? Yes, IV *can* offer learner-control and discovery-learning in a superb way, but it does a lot of other things very well, too.' (Dr Keith Roach, a reader of a draft version of this Guide.)

National Interactive Video Centre

The National Interactive Video Centre (27 Marylebone Road, London NW1 5JS) is sponsored by the Department of Trade and Industry, the Manpower Services

Commission, Philips Electronics, and Thorn EMI, and is administered by the Council for Educational Technology. Staff at the Centre can give further information and advice about the applications of interactive video.

PRACTICAL KITS

Much of the following is drawn from the very helpful description of practical kits in the Open University, written by Greenfield (see Booklist).

Points for

Ingenious kits can save the learner the inconvenience of attending a centre.

Help learner to interact with future working environment.

Motivate learners.

Can be cheap and easy to put together.

May be the only way certain objectives can be achieved.

Can look exciting.

Points against

A good kit is a major design challenge — ie, a kit that is relevant, attractive and robust.

Kit avoidance; learners may ignore kits, seeing them as less important than more conventional media such as print.

Some equipment is inaccurate and unsophisticated.

Learners get frustrated when things go wrong.

Can be expensive and elaborate to produce.

Some kits are big and inconvenient, eg, to transport.

Storage, packaging, post, insurance and maintenance can present problems

Can look daunting.

Uses

Change of activity.

For practical/manual skills and applications.

For developing initiative.

Demonstrates that there is a valid link between theory and practice.

For discovery learning.

Examples

Plymouth electronics kit (textbook, study guide, microprocessor).

Many and varied Open University kits, eg, 220 items in S101 kit (Science foundation course); pickled sheep's brain for biology course; some are very expensive (eg, microprocessor kit); some very cheap (eg, straws and a tabletennis ball).

Southtek kits include a simulation of an automatic washing machine cycle for electronics students.

Notes

Consider all costs, for example:

— to develop the kit
— to buy the components
— to maintain the kit (preparing, checking, servicing, replacing)
— to store and distribute the kit.

Careful design of activities and backup elsewhere in the package can minimize the disadvantages (eg, of inaccurate equipment).

Support material is almost always necessary, eg, to instruct the learner in how to use the kit (time, procedures, components).

A kit used in Australia 'proved so successful with external students that it was subsequently adapted for use by on-campus students. Normal laboratory sessions were superseded by an "open" laboratory in which students worked independently with the kit under guidance from an audiotape' (Rowntree, 1981, p 158).

BROADCAST RADIO AND TELEVISION

Points for

Available to all the population — broadcast potentially into every home; reaches the isolated.

Good at raising awareness.

Free to the educationalist to use.

Prestigious, good 'image'.

See too the advantages of video, page 90.

Points against

Transmission times of programmes are often very awkward.

Programming details are often released too late for educational planners to plan related provision.

Lack of earmarked air-time for educational/training organizations.

Viewers/listeners tend to view these media as 'entertainment', use them passively (applies to tutors as well as learners).

Learners often need *persuading* to use broadcast radio and television for study purposes.

Linear — continuous and fixed presentation.

Transient — few, if any, repeats.

See note on video (page 84).

Not always easy to relate to local/individual need, tends to be aimed at the average viewer.

Poor at catering for minorities.

Uses

To stimulate learners.

To support and enrich existing courses.

For broadcast television — see also video (page 84).

Can present the learner with examples (eg, field experiments) that are impossible to gain in any other way.

Examples

The best-known example of broadcast radio and television is the Open University.

Other examples are series which have learning materials and other provision built around them — eg, literacy and numeracy programmes, programmes on languages and economics — and the most striking of all — the BBC Computer Literacy project, which is described in Volume 1, *Open Learning in Action*.

These models are much more likely to be developed over the next 20 years than the OU model.

Notes

Good planning uses strengths of these media and compensates for their weaknesses by other means such as additional media for the package and extra support.

The potential for linking with independent local radio stations has hardly been developed yet.

On their own, broadcast programmes cannot easily develop practical skills.

Note on cable and satellite transmission

It is unlikely that any organization other than the Open University could afford to use either BBC, ITV or Channel 4 to broadcast course-related material. On the other hand, those companies may well produce extremely good programmes which link in with open-learning courses (Channel 4's 'A question of economics' leading to a BTEC or Scottish National Certificate is a good example).

Of much greater educational potential in the long term is cable television and/or direct broadcasting by satellite. These can be more flexible, more locally responsive, cheaper and more interactive than conventional broadcasting.

Cable, with its local franchise areas and commitment to provide educational content, could offer more specialized educational material for use by open-learning students or for use by a large educational provider. Cable can also distribute digital information as well as sound and pictures. This would enable computer programs and data to be transmitted at the same time.

A note on the advantages of videocassettes over broadcast television

BROADCAST TELEVISION	VIDEOCASSETTE
Ephemeral	Permanent, available when required
Fixed timing for transmission	Can be used at learner's convenience
Fixed structure — linear, runs from start to finish	Learner/tutor can interrupt, stop the cassette, eg, for discussion or note-taking; can move on or back in the tape; can move to/from other elements in the learning package

There are two sorts of videocassette. Firstly, the recording of a programme made initially for broadcast transmission. Secondly, a programme prepared specifically for cassette use. If the latter, it is possible to structure the material for interactive use, eg, short sequences with questions and activities. In this case clear cues must be given to the learner on what to do (eg, when to stop) and good documentation is needed of what is on the cassette.

VIDEOTEX
Introduction
Terminology can be confusing. 'Videotex' is the generic term, covering teletext and viewdata. These latter two terms are defined below; see also the Glossary.

Teletext
Information broadcast, decoded and displayed on a television screen or visual display unit. One frame is presented after another in a repeated cycle. ('Teletext': text transmitted by television.)

Viewdata
Information transmitted via a telephone line from a central computer using specific codings and conventions for display on a television set or VDU, allowing interactive communication, such as telebanking or teleshopping. PRESTEL is an example of such a system.

Microviewdata (sometimes called local viewdata)
Software allowing users to create viewdata pages and databases themselves, using a microcomputer. The more sophisticated software packages enable other people to gain access to such databases, via the telephone line.

TELETEXT
For more information than is given below, see *Teletext Systems* by P Zorkoczy, in the Booklist.

Points for
Almost immediate delivery of pages.

Cheap (uses existing television receiver).

Software can be downloaded.

Provides colourful display, user-friendly.

Page storage possible on disc if using microcomputer.

Points against
Not in itself an interactive medium.

One-way transmission of information.

Number of pages is very limited unless full bandwidth utilized.

Television screen is not good to learn from, ie, when displaying pages of text in isolation.

Controlled by non-educational/training authorities so far.

Currently mostly limited to news, information and entertainment.

Television requires teletext decoder.

Uses
To provide information.

Tests or questions related to a course.

Subtitles for broadcast television.

To update other materials (eg, print).

A useful adjunct to other materials.

Examples
CEEFAX has an educational telesoftware project under way.

Notes
Software simulating teletext pages can be purchased.

VIEWDATA
Viewdata, for example PRESTEL, enables a user to call up a remote database, and to access data by using a modified television set plus a keypad, or a microcomputer plus modem. The user can thus access information held on a remote computer, by using a telephone line.

Points for
PRESTEL is nationwide and open 24 hours. (Some small, specialized databases operate for only part of the day.)

Wide access.

Easy to use and to update.

Colourful, user-friendly; like watching television.

Own-pace learning possible.

Security restrictions (can restrict access to certain pages, eg, to particular learner groups).

Vast storage of information; very large database.

Downloading of software and of data.

Electronic mail facility (but limited message length).

Page storage for review/future use (if using microcomputer).

Printout facility makes it possible to check learning.

Central record-keeping (individual performance).

Local-call access via PRESTEL to 96 per cent of users.

Telesoftware capabilities.

Teletransactions are possible, eg, home banking, teleshopping, investment portfolio management.

Gateway potential into other databases.

Points against
Equipment can be expensive (but cheap modems available for popular microcomputers).

Very limited training material available (but see Beck and Burton, and Burton and Taylor in the Booklist).

Only simple graphics.

Limited interactivity (except when remote databases are accessed via a gateway).

Small viewdata systems may have limited number of users.

Occasional interference (telephone line noise).

Incurs charges whenever used.

Tree structure can be slow to locate relevant part of database.

Uses
Updating information where rapid change of technology.

Large organizations, eg, banks who already have the facilities.

Wide-scale geographic distribution.

One-to-one use using MAILBOX facility. (Sometimes with limited copying facility.)

Accessing databases.

Examples
Barclays Bank Training Centre.

British Medical Journal doctors' case-studies.

Many organizations, large and small, use the public viewdata system, for 'publishing' information and for directing it at specific users. In addition, several large organizations have their own private viewdata systems, either accessed through

PRESTEL or BT Gold, or in a completely separate landline system. These private systems are used for data transfer (eg, salesmen sending in the day's orders via telephone link) and for training (eg, Thomas Cook).

Notes
There is a difference between a public viewdata system such as PRESTEL and private systems which can be run in-company or to a limited audience.

Private systems can be set up relatively cheaply and avoid PRESTEL registration charges, etc.

TELETUTORING
Introduction
The telephone can be used for two purposes in an open-learning scheme: to provide advice, help and counselling, and to transmit actual course material. The first of these purposes is discussed in Volume 3, *How to Tutor and Support Learners*. This section considers the second use, ie, where learners are taught wholly or partly by means of the telephone.

Other media may or may not be used; the telephone link may be used for mainstream material or only for remedial/enrichment purposes. The telephone tutoring may be live or prepackaged.

The use of the telephone for tutoring, as opposed to support, is relatively uncommon in the UK. It is more widely used abroad, for example as a means of providing updating for doctors and other professionals.

The following points are elaborated by George and Robinson (see the Booklist).

Points for
Good at:

— passing information
— generating ideas
— problem-solving
— asking questions
— exchanging ideas
— cognitive areas.

It can offer a degree of personal support to the learner.

A high percentage of the population has telephone access.

The medium is familiar.

It can be cheaper and quicker to prepare telephone courses than courses in other media.

Points against
It is difficult:

— to exchange highly technical or visual information
— to persuade people to establish a relationship
— to use for development of some interpersonal skills.

Some BT exchange lines give excessive interference.

Uses

Support and communication of information supplementary to the package.

Can bring learners together in 'conference'.

Examples

Argyll and Bute Home Study courses offer only conference call support.

Notes

Conference calls are more widely used in the UK for support than for teaching.

The technology of electronic 'bridges', which link learners together, is improving.

Tutors need to adapt when using the telephone in this way. They lack face-to-face feedback from the learners; they have to prepare more carefully than they may be used to and there is a danger that the tutor will exert too tight a control. Also, the tutor has to make allowance for the inability of the medium to transmit illustrative material (drawings, diagrams, graphics) (but see Cyclops below).

See Job Aid 6 (p 113) for a checklist for tutor.

CYCLOPS

Introduction

Cyclops was designed to overcome the lack of a graphics mode when using the telephone as a medium for teaching. Cyclops is a collection of hardware (computer, cassette recorder, lightpen, software) that enables the tutor to draw in colour on the television screen, to generate text and to edit. He can either prepare material in advance *or* send the video pictures down a standard telephone line, to be decoded back into pictures on a television screen at the other end. Up to six learners in separate locations can be taught in this way at any one time. All concerned can see — and modify — what is on the screen. They can all hear one another. Cyclops is described in 'In the comfort of your own campus' by A W Bates (*The Times Higher Educational Supplement,* 9.11.84), and in 'Cyclops: shared screen teleconferencing' by David McConnell in Bates, A W, *The role of training in distance education.*

The advantages, disadvantages and uses of Cyclops are set out below.

Points for

Extends range of telephone tutoring.

Offers writing/drawing facility.

Interactive — learners are *involved,* eg, in labelling apparatus in an experiment.

Easier to prepare tutoring material than for, say, broadcast television.

User-friendly tutoring.

Low cost.

The tutor does not have to acquire complex skills.

Use of cassette frees the tutor to talk.

Points against
Some training needed for tutors.

Learners will not be familiar with this way of learning.

Learners have to attend a centre (equipment is not yet in the home).

Lack of certain visual characteristics; the material on the screen can be jointly viewed but participants cannot see one another.

Early models needed two telephone lines for audio and video contact. This restricted the use of CYCLOPS.

Uses
Diagrams can be constructed from scratch.

Learners can erase, eg, creating a communal set of notes.

Examples
Mainly in Open University and in an OU/schools pilot study (see McConnell in the Booklist).

Note
See note opposite on the way tutors need to adjust to telephone tutoring.

CONCLUSION
The obvious medium for most open-learning packages is print. You'll have seen that there are good reasons for this. But we hope you will consider other media as well because

— print cannot do everything
— a variety of media can stimulate the learner and reinforce learning
— a variety of media can make the package more attractive and help you to market it
— learners' expectations move on. Technology develops, costs change, and open-learning providers ought to keep pace.

You do, though, have to take decisions carefully, because using a range of media

— increases cost
— limits the flexibility of the package in use
— makes the package more complex.

An example from the Open Tech Programme
EETPU, the electricians' union, is cooperating with a communications software company to produce interactive videodiscs on new technology. The discs will allow learners to work at their own pace through the material and define and satisfy their own training needs. The overall development costs, however, will be £150,000 (1984 prices) and the materials will be available only at the union's college in Cudham, where the hardware will be located. A less expensive system could have

been delivered locally or regionally for home-based/work-based study but the high degree of individualization and interactivity would have been lost. We can imagine the debate that took place over the various options available.

FOR VIDEODISC	AGAINST VIDEODISC
This system will enable our members to define their own training needs. They will be able to fill in the gaps in their knowledge and update themselves as and when appropriate.	We have fantastic development costs. Once these discs are mastered it will be difficult to change them for years.
Our members have such vastly different learning needs in the field of new technology that any package other than videodisc would prove unsatisfactory to the vast majority of learners. To some it would be too basic, to others far too sophisticated.	Let us go for portable packages with print and audio tapes, freely available for training in groups or for home-based learning throughout the UK.
The core concepts will not change; the discs will last a few years and by the time they need replacing the cost of videodisc technology will have tumbled to the point where re-investment will be cost effective.	This will cost us a lot in every way — money, time and hassle. We could make something available much more quickly, and make an impact, by using simpler media.
The important thing to alter will be the computer software not the disc and this is comparatively easy.	The added expense of hardware (both needing a computer *and* a videodisc player) dramatically limits where people can use the materials.
As the cost falls the hardware will become freely available up and down the country.	Most of our members can get access to a video-cassette player. We can get all the benefits of colour and movement by building in a videotape element to the package.
Anyway we can probably sell a number of packages to other centres and recoup some of the development cost.	

Cynics will point out that the careful analysis may have been weighted in the end by the availability of public funding. At the time, the Department of Trade and Industry was partly financing developments in videodisc packages. It is not of course unusual for one issue to dominate the selection of medium. The enthusiasm of one influential person for a particular medium is another example of the same phenomenon.

Q | **Quiz**
1. Tick the two statements from the following that accord with the material presented in this section.

(a) Prestel is an example of a viewdata system.

(b) There are several open-learning schemes in the UK which manage entirely without printed material.

(c) Learners are often reluctant to use broadcast television as a medium for serious study.

(d) Audiocassette players are not widely enough available so a course designer would be unwise to build audiotape into a scheme of home-based open learning.

2. Match up the items in the two columns, eg, if you think video is well suited to the development of manual skills you would match (a) with (i).

(a) video	(i) well suited to the development of manual skills
(b) computer	(ii) shows movement — normal speed, speeded up or slowed down
(c) practical kits	(iii) a powerful medium for managing learning as well as presenting course material.

Answers

1. (a) and (c) are correct.

Here are some comments on the other options.

(b) There may be, but the authors do not know of them.

(d) Tony Bates reckoned that if 80 per cent or more of learners in your target group own, or will buy, the relevant hardware you can reasonably use that medium. The figure quoted for 1990 is 90 per cent ownership of audiocassette recorders. Even now (1985) you could almost certainly justify the use of audiocassettes in nearly every case, so widespread is the hardware.

2. (a) and (ii): (b) and (iii); (c) and (i).

Other answers are remotely possible, for example, some practical kits may make (ii) possible. Other combinations are wrong, for example (a) and (i): video is generally agreed to be ill suited to developing practical skills unless it is computer-controlled (as in interactive video), when it may also be good at (iii).

Part Three, Job Aids, Checklists, Booklist and Glossary

Section One. Job Aids

CONTENTS
Introduction
Job aid 1. Reviewing open-learning materials: a checklist
Job aid 2. An alternative checklist
Job aid 3. Criteria for open-learning materials
Job aid 4. Matrix for selecting media
Job aid 5. A flow diagram for media selection
Job aid 6. Teleconferencing: a checklist for tutors

INTRODUCTION

This section includes six job aids which will help you implement the suggestions and ideas contained in this book. The first three relate to Part One of this book, the second three (job aids 4, 5 and 6) relate to Part Two.

Job aid 1 is an extensive checklist from which you can select questions relevant to your own search for materials.

Job aid 2 is a shorter list of questions to help in the process of selecting packages.

Job aid 3 is a list of the fundamental characteristics of open-learning materials, drawn up by MARIS.

Job aid 4 is a matrix to help you consider each medium from a number of different points of view.

Job aid 5 is a flow diagram to help you select appropriate media.

Job aid 6 is a checklist for those using the telephone as a medium for tutoring.

You should also refer to the checklists which follow this section. These checklists can also be used as job aids.

JOB AID 1. REVIEWING OPEN-LEARNING MATERIALS: A CHECKLIST

This job aid is intended to give you ideas for devising your own checklist. You should not use it slavishly. You will need to use only those categories that make sense in your own context. It is based on similar lists produced by CET and included, in a modified form, in Coombe Lodge Working Paper 1606, *Learning Materials for Open Learning in Further Education* (Latcham, 1981). Reference is made below to other volumes in the Open Learning Guides series, if you need fuller information or fuller checklists on any category.

1. General

How long will it take to process an order?

What is the cost? Any discounts?

Are there any particular copyright implications?

What updating service is available from the supplier (eg, details of new packages, information on syllabus changes)?

What is the date of first publication? Has the content been recently revised?

2. Purpose of package

(See Volume 2, *How to Help Learners Assess Their Progress*, and Volume 6, *How to Communicate with the Learner.*)

For whom was the package written?

Will this package suit the learners in our scheme? Consider: level of package, skills, experience, attitude.

What syllabus, skill, qualification, etc, was the package prepared for?

Are the objectives stated clearly for the learner?

Are there any prerequisites?

3. Elements in the package

(See Volume 6, *How to Communicate with the Learner* and this volume (8), *How to Find and Adapt Materials and Select Media.*) Does the package include

— specially written open-learning text
— handbook/guide to the package
— textbooks
— audiotape(s)
— videotape(s)
— practical kit
— computer tape/disc
— other?

Is a clear description given of the package?

What additional equipment would be needed to use the package? Consider: a library, laboratory, a computer, a video player.

Are there guidance notes for tutors?

4. Structure of the package

(See Volume 6, *How to Communicate with the Learner.*)

How is the package divided? Consider: modules, units, chapters, segments, etc.

Is an approximate study time given for each division of the package?

What aids are provided

— at the start of each section (eg, introduction; list of objectives; list of equipment needed)
— during each section (eg, symbols to indicate practical activities; self-assessment questions)
— at the end of each section (eg, summaries, checklists, things to do next).

Are format features clearly and attractively signalled?

5. Assessment
(See Volume 2, *How to Help Learners Assess Their Progress.*)

Is there sufficient opportunity for the learner to assess his own progress, ie, are there sufficient

— self-assessment questions
— activities
— exercises
— pre-tests
— post-tests?

Is sufficient feedback given in the package?

Are there teacher/trainer assessment questions?

Is there a teacher/trainer assessment guide?

Is the assessment

— balanced
— varied
— relevant to the objectives?

6. Teaching approach
(See Volume 2, *How to Help Learners Assess Their Progress,* and Volume 6, *How to Communicate With the Learner.*)

Is the method of presenting the subject clear and logical?

Does the method sufficiently involve the learner?

Is good use made of any tutor/trainer?

Is the material well structured?

Is the sequencing sound?

Is good use made of the medium/media?

7. Subject matter
(See Volume 6, *How to Communicate With the Learner.*)

Is the content accurate? Up to date?

Does the selection and content suit the objectives?

Are any objectives missed?

Is any content redundant?

Is the learner adequately prepared for any syllabus, etc?

Are difficult ideas/processes sufficiently unpacked?

8. Presentation
(See Volume 6, *How to Communicate with the Learner,* and Volume 7, *How to Manage the Production Process.*)

Is the package easy to handle and use?

Is it attractive (whether print, tape or whatever)?

Is it durable?

Is it well illustrated?

Is the language accessible?

Is the standard of reproduction acceptable (whether print, sound or vision)?

Is page layout attractive?

Are headings clear?

Are the open-learning features clearly and consistently indicated?

Is there space for learner notes?

Is colour used to good effect?

9. Package support

(See Volume 2, *How to Help Learners Assess Their Progress*, and Volume 6, *How to Communicate With the Learner.*)

Will the learner need any extra support in order to study the package, eg

— tutorials
— pre-course counselling
— in-course counselling
— facilities for practical work
— facilities to sit an examination
— access to a library?

10. Closing questions

Will the package fit into our scheme? If not, is the package sufficiently good for us to modify either it or the scheme?

Will the package suit our learners and tutors?

Is the package

Suitable as it stands?	Suitable with minor adaptations?	Suitable with more substantial change?	OK as ancillary resource, eg, in a library?	Not usable?

JOB AID 2. AN ALTERNATIVE CHECKLIST
An alternative checklist is shown opposite. It is extracted from *Supported Self-Study: a handbook for teachers,* by Philip Waterhouse, Council for Educational Technology, 1983, and is intended for use in schools' contexts.

EVALUATION OF A STRUCTURED COURSE   **WORKING PAPER 2**

This form could be used by a course team that is planning or reviewing a self-study programme. It focuses on the suitability of a structured course which is intended to form the core of the learning materials. The form should be completed independently by each team member, and then the results could be used as a basis for discussion. The evaluation consists of a number of assertions. The judgement of the team member should be indicated in the box according to the following scale: 1 = agree; 2 = partly agree; 3 = disagree.

1. There is a reasonably clear statement of objectives at the start of each section of the course. ☐

2. The text is sufficiently well-divided into manageable blocks to make reading and comprehension easier. ☐

3. Typography, particularly in the headings and subheadings, is helpful to the reader. ☐

4. There is a use of graphics to help in explanations of difficult concepts. ☐

5. The sequencing of ideas and tasks is helpful to the learner. ☐

6. The reading level of the material is within the capabilities of our target group. ☐

7. The written material is concise and free of verbosity. ☐

8. The language is not unnecessarily clouded with academic jargon. ☐

9. Pupil tasks occur at sufficiently regular intervals for the pupil's interest to be maintained. ☐

10. The self-assessment questions are suitable for self-study situations. ☐

11. Answers to self-assessment questions are provided. ☐

12. There is a good selection of problems and assignments for teacher marking. ☐

13. The whole package seems within the capability of our target group of learners. ☐

14. The package is attractive to look at and to use. ☐

15. There is a list of useful references for additional material. ☐

JOB AID 3. CRITERIA FOR OPEN-LEARNING MATERIALS

This list was produced by MARIS in 1984.

Attractive (eg, spacious presentation, informal tone, easy to handle, well packaged).

Well structured (eg, clear links between different media, objectives clearly stated, headings, overview and summaries provided; adequate signposting between sections).

Interactive (eg, activities provided for the learner, dialogue with the learner, hands-on experience).

Related to experience of the learner (eg, relevant outcomes are clearly identified).

Built-in self-assessment (eg, tests or other devices together with feedback that enable the learner to assess his/her performance/degree of success).

JOB AID 4. MATRIX FOR SELECTING MEDIA

Medium	Purchase costs	Production costs	Time to produce	Reproduction costs	Storage, distribution costs	Maintenance costs	Updating costs
Print							
Audiotape							
Slide/tape							
Video							
Computer							
Interactive video							
Practical kits							
Broadcast radio and TV							
Teletext							
Viewdata							
Telephone							

Notes

It is possible to break down each factor further as in the checklist entries (see page 115).

Or you may choose fewer factors, depending on your context.

You may also subdivide the media (eg, instead of PRINT use BOOK, RING BINDER, PAMPHLET) and/or use combinations (eg, AUDIO/PRINT).

You may fill in the matrix by using any system of your own, eg, ticks (for strong) and crosses (for weak), scoring from 1 = excellent down to 5 = unusable. Or you may decide to write brief notes in the boxes.

Once you have completed the matrix for all relevant media you should be able to sum up the advantages and disadvantages of each, *for your particular use.*

For a more elaborate approach see Holden, E F J, in the Booklist.

Costs to learner	Ease of use	Ease of access	Degree of learner control	Accept-ability to learner	Accept-ability to tutor trainer	Suit-ability to sub matter/ objectives	Inter-activity

JOB AID 5. A FLOW DIAGRAM FOR MEDIA SELECTION

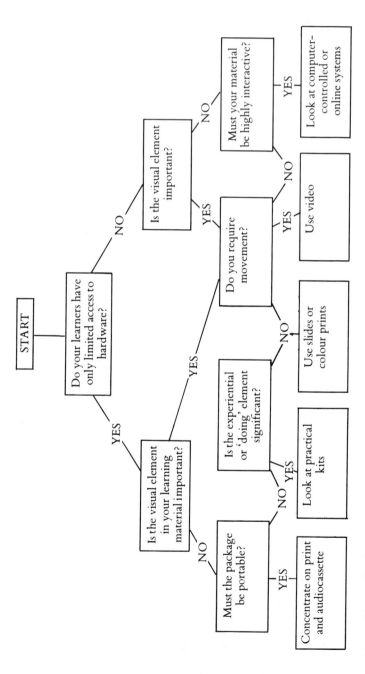

Note: this is offered as one way of considering media selection. It will often need adaptation and extension to suit particular circumstances.

Before the teleconference

Has a welcome letter been sent to learners confirming the conference?

Have brief biographies of those taking part been circulated (if necessary)?

Have participants been given details of

— how to join the call
— how to operate the equipment
— what to do if in difficulties (eg, a bad line)?

Has an agenda been drawn up? Are items given approximate timings?

Have objectives for the conference been defined?

Have any necessary materials been sent in advance to participants?

Has the format of the conference been made clear (eg, discussion, questions and answer)?

Does this format provide sufficient variety?

Has the tutor prepared for the conference (eg, has he planned answers to a range of questions he may be asked)?

Has follow-up work been planned?

Has a questionnaire been included in the participants' mailing, to evaluate the call?

During the teleconference

Does the chairman welcome everyone in a friendly way?

Are the participants introduced to one another?

Is information given on how to use the equipment?

Are general rules for participation made clear (eg, can participants interrupt or should they wait to be asked)?

Are individuals addressed by name?

Are individuals asked to give their name before making a contribution?

Is the agenda followed? Are times kept to?

Do all the learners participate fully? Is everything possible done to achieve this? Are specific individuals asked for their comments?

Are participants asked to lead on any topics?

Is the format of the conference varied (eg, short sequences; changes of activity and pace)?

Are supporting materials used to maximum effect?

After the teleconference

Is an evaluation sheet used to get participants' comments on the conference?

Is other follow-up material arranged (eg, telephone contact with one or more participants to discuss how the conference went)?

Is the feedback used to plan the next conference?

Is a summary of the conference sent to all participants?

For discussion on these and other topics, and for a draft evaluation sheet see Grimwade, J R, in the Booklist. Write also to PACNET (the Plymouth Audioconferencing Network) at Plymouth Polytechnic, Drake Circus, Plymouth, PL4 8AA, for details of their teleconferencing service and their training materials.

Section Two. Checklists

The following checklist sections refer to the headings in the matrix in job aid 4 (page 110).

COSTS

Purchase costs
Can you purchase what you need off the shelf (see Part One of this book)?

Production costs/time
Are you producing the package from scratch?

How much will this cost? Have you the budget for this?

Have you relevant hardware, facilities and other resources to make the package?

Will your staff need training?

Will you be using subcontractors?

What will the subcontractors do?

What will the subcontractors cost?

Are the responsibilities of members of the production team clearly defined?

What is your production schedule?

How much lead time is necessary?

What documentation will you need to maintain whilst making the package?

When will you pilot?

Will you be marketing the package? Will it be easily marketable in the medium you have chosen?

See the checklists in Volume 7, *How to Manage the Production Process*, for more details on production.

Reproduction costs
Are reproduction costs reasonable?

Storage, distribution costs
Will there be costs involved in

— storage
— distribution
— handling?

How will these costs be met?

Maintenance costs
What responsibilities will you have to service hardware and software?

Have you adequate arrangements to meet these responsibilities?

How reliable is the hardware and software?

Updating costs
Will the software be easy to update or otherwise adapt?

Who will be responsible for updating?

Costs to learner
Will costs to the learner be realistic?

What will learners have to buy?

What will others (eg, employers) have to provide for the learner?

EASE OF USE
Is the medium (hardware and software) portable? Does it need to be?

Is the equipment easy to set up and operate?

Will the learner be able to use the equipment without supervision?

EASE OF ACCESS
Will learners be able to use the package at a place convenient to them?

Have learners access to appropriate hardware?

Is this access difficult or costly to arrange?

Will the learner be able to use the equipment whenever he wishes?

DEGREE OF LEARNER CONTROL
Is the package easy for the learner to control (both hardware and software)?

Can the learner easily find what he wants?

ACCEPTABILITY TO LEARNER
Will the package appeal to the learner?

Have the learners' expectations, skills, interests and experience all been fully considered?

ACCEPTABILITY TO TUTOR/TRAINER
Will the tutor/trainer find the medium acceptable?

Do you need to produce any material specially for the tutor/trainer?

SUITABILITY FOR SUBJECT MATTER/OBJECTIVES

How suitable is the medium for the subject/skill?

How suitable is the medium for the objectives of the course?

INTERACTIVITY

Can the interactive features of open learning easily be built into the medium?

Section Three. Booklist

Bates, A W (ed), *The Role of Technology in Distance Education*, Croom Helm/St Martins Press, 1984. This is a collection of essays, many of which are referred to in this book and thus listed separately in this Booklist.

Bates, A W, 'Broadcast television' in the above.

Bates, A W, 'In the comfort of your own campus', *The Times Higher Educational Supplement*, 9 November 1984.

Bates, A W, 'Resources for learning, *The Times Educational Supplement*, 20 April 1984.

Bates, A W, 'Learning from audio visual media', 33–58, *Institutional Research Review, No. 1, Student Learning from Different Media in the Open University*, Spring 1982.

Bayard-White, C, *Interactive Video Case Studies and Directory*, National Interactive Video Centre, 1985.

Beck, J and Burton, J, *Prestel and Microviewdata in Education: a training course*, Council for Educational Technology, 1985. The eight modules can be combined to provide the basis of a two- or three-day workshop or they can be presented as a series of evening sessions.

Burton, J and Taylor, J, *Educational Viewdata: start-up and user guides*, Council for Educational Technology, 1985. These materials comprise two guides and an accompanying disc of viewdata examples.

Council for Educational Technology, Information Sheet 6, 'Copyright', CET, 1984 comprising:
(i) 'The use of copyright printed material for educational purposes'
(ii) 'Copyright and the copying of sound recordings for educational purposes'
(iii) 'Copyright and computers'
(iv) 'Off-air recording of broadcast programmes for educational purposes'
(v) 'Protection of computer programs'
(vi) 'Copyright and the copying of films'
This CET publication provides a useful guide and summary of the current position.

Council for Educational Technology, Information Sheet 7, 'Teleconferencing', CET, 1983.

Council for Educational Technology, Information Sheet 10, 'Videotext', CET, 1985

Council for Educational Technology, Information Sheet 12, 'Supported Self-Study', CET, 1985

Construction Industry Training Board, *Computer Assisted Training*, Management Training Series XA 618. A refreshingly simple, practical introduction to the topic.

Crabb, Geoffrey, *Copyright Agreements between Employers and Staff in Education*, Council for Educational Technology, 1979 (free)

Crabb, Geoffrey, *Copyright Clearance: a practical guide*, (Guideline 2), Council for Educational Technology, 1981. This is the most readable and comprehensive guide to copyright.

Dean, C and Whitlock, Q, *A Handbook of Computer-Based Training*, Kogan Page, 1983. This is a standard text.

Dean, C and Whitlock, Q, 'Computer-based training' in *The Personnel and Training Databook*, Kogan Page, 1983

Doulton, A and Bayard-White, C, *Interactive Video*, National Interactive Video Centre, 1985. A simple, clear introduction to the subject.

Duchastel, P, 'Unbounded text' in *Educational Technology*, XXII, *8*, August 1982. This article suggests setting text on sheets 23 × 33 in (map size). One chapter of a book (12–16 pp) could go on this. The article discusses the advantages this gives (eg, enables the learner to overview, gives design flexibility) and disadvantages (eg, difficulty of keeping the sheets together).

Duchastel, P, 'Towards the ideal study guide', *British Journal of Educational Technology*, 14, *3*, October 1983. This covers (1) the function of a study guide (orientation, task direction, learning assistance, self-assessment); (2) study guide components — purpose, significance and goals; text reference; outline of the subject matter; questions on the subject matter; key words and phrases; application problem, assignment test — a self-administered quiz. A very helpful article.

Duke, J, *Interactive video: implications for education and training* (Working Paper 22), Council for Educational Technology, 1983. The first major publication on interactive video, now inevitably somewhat dated.

Durbridge, N, 'Audio cassettes' in Bates, A W (ed), 1984 (see above).

Evans, T, 'Communicating with students by audiotape' in *Teaching at a Distance, 25*, Open University, Autumn 1984. One of a number of useful articles on media selection appearing in this journal.

Ferguson, C T, *New Learning Systems: some Canadian approaches*, Coombe Lodge Report 15, *8*, the Further Education Staff College, Coombe Lodge, Blagdon, Bristol, BS18 6RG, 1982.

Geisert, Paul and Futrell, Mynga, 'Evaluating classroom computer courseware'. Details available from Paul Geisert, 1158 5th Street, NE, Washington, DC. Offers useful checklists.

George, J, *On the Line*, Open University Centre for Continuing Education. Available from the Learning Material Service, Centre for Continuing Education, PO Box 188, Milton Keynes MK3 6HW. A practical guide.

Greenfield, D, 'Practical kits' in Bates, A W (ed), 1984 (see above).

Grimwade, J R, 'Issues in teleconferencing' in *Open Campus*, ISSN 0812 061. Referred to in job aid 6.

Harris, D, *Preparing Educational Materials*, Croom Helm, 1979. This has a chapter on 'Modes of learning', which compares the various media.

Heidt, E U, *Instructional Media and the Individual Learner*, Kogan Page, 1978. A standard text on media.

Holden, E F J, 'Selection of instructional media systems' in *Programmed Learning and Educational Technology* 12.5, September 1975. Referred to in job aid 4.

International Extension College, *Administration of Distance Teaching Institutions*, IEC, 1983. Unit 4, pp 50–60 on the production of radio/audio recordings covers (for example) stages of broadcast production, decisions on content, production methods.

Jones, Ann, 'Computer-assisted learning in distance education' in Bates, A W (ed), 1984 (see above).

Knapper, C K, *Evaluating Instructional Technology*, Croom Helm, 1980. This compares various media.

Latcham, J, *Learning Materials for Open Learning in Further Education*, Coombe Lodge Working Paper 1606, 1981. Available from FE Staff College, Coombe Lodge, Blagdon, Bristol, BS18 6RG.

Laurillard, D M, *The Problems and Possibilities of Interactive Video*, IET Paper No. 223. Reprinted in *New Technologies for Distance Education*, O'Shea, T, *et al* (eds), Harvester Press (forthcoming). This article gives a fascinating analysis of the potential of interactive video. It outlines the ideal self-learning situation — the informal, relaxed way in which we find things out. Interactive video has the potential to simulate this non-formal learning situation; the learner can use his own idiosyncratic way of asking questions, locating information and deciding sequence. *But* educators and trainers will have to organize material to facilitate this. At the moment much interactive video design is based on the trainer-directed tradition of computer-based training.

Laurillard, D M, *Interactive video and the control of learning*, IET Papers on Broadcasting 231. Published in *Educational Technology 236*, 1984.

Lewis, R, *How to Write Self-study Materials*, Council for Educational Technology, 1981. A simple, accessible guide to the topic.

Lewis, R, *How to Tutor in an Open-Learning Scheme*, Council for Educational Technology, 1981. Available in both individual and group versions.

Lister, P, *The Coventry Computer-Based Learning Project*, the report of the steering group of the Coventry Computer-Based Learning Project using Plato, Manpower Services Commission, December 1983. This contains many useful insights and is, at the time of writing, available free from MSC, Moorfoot, Sheffield, S1 4PQ.

McConnell, D, 'Cyclops shared-screen teleconferencing' in Bates, A W (ed), 1984 (see above).

Morris, A, *Writing Study Guides*, Council for Educational Technology, 1984. An alternative approach to writing study guides to that taken in this Guide.

National Computer Centre, CBT Library Module 3, CBT Case Histories, NCC, 1983. This series of NCC modules is an important source for readers wishing to keep up to date with computer-based training.

Open University, *How to Develop Self-Instructional Teaching*, 1979. A course for developing distance-learning materials aimed mainly at an international market.

Paine, N, 'Which button do I push?' (the use of video in open learning) in *Distance No Object*, HMSO, 1982.

Paine, N, 'Information technology' in Tucker, J (ed) *Educational Training and the New Technologies*, Kogan Page, 1984.

Paine, N, 'Information technology using open learning: the interactivity analogue' in Shaw, K E (ed), *Aspects of Educational Technology XVII*, Kogan Page, 1984. These three articles by Nigel Paine elaborate points made in the section of this book that deals with newer media.

Parsloe, E, *Interactive Video*, Sigma Technical Press, 1984. A useful compendium of information on all aspects of interactive video including the technical.

Robinson, B, 'Telephone teaching' in Bates, A W (ed), 1984 (see above).

Rogers, Wendy Stainton, 'The alternative use of Open University learning materials', internal Open University document. This article describes transformation (take bits from original materials and alter them, eg, by using different media); selection (use only bits of the original); augmentation (generate new materials to cover local circumstances); integration (weld together the adapted package). A revised version of this paper appeared in *Teaching at a Distance* No. 24, Autumn 1983, as 'The uses of materials', but this unfortunately omitted many of the more interesting points from the original Open University paper.

Romiszowski, A G, *The Selection and Use of Instructional Media*, Kogan Page, 1977. Very solid if somewhat over-elaborated.

Rowntree, D, *Developing Courses for Students*, McGraw-Hill, 1981. This book has useful sections on media choice.

Schramm, W, *Big Media, Little Media*, Sage, Beverly Hills, 1977. A standard source.

Thompson, V, Brown, C, Knowles, C, *Videotex in Education: a new technology briefing*, Council for Educational Technology, 1982.

Training Officer, The, Audio Visual Aids in Training, Marylebone Press, 1982. This selection of articles from *The Training Officer* gives much practical advice on how to make and use such media as audiocassette, video and the overhead projector.

Waterhouse, Philip, *Managing the Learning Process*, McGraw-Hill, 1983. An important work for those working in schools.

Waterhouse, Philip, *Preparing Assignments in Supported Self-Study*, Occasional Paper 3, Council for Educational Technology, February 1984, Also very important for those working in schools. Available from Philip Waterhouse, 8 Copse Road, Keynsham, Bristol BS18 1TH.

Wellington, J, 'Aid to intuition', *The Times Educational Supplement*, 18 May 1984. A useful checklist for selecting software.

Winders, R, 'The Plymouth Audioconferencing Network' in *Teaching at a Distance* No. 25, Autumn 1984. This article describes PACNET. PACNET (the Plymouth Audioconferencing Network) is also at the time of writing — April 1985 — beginning to produce some useful training material for teleconferencing. Contact Ray Winders, Director, PACNET, Learning Resources Centre, Plymouth Polytechnic, Drake Circus, Plymouth, PL4 8AA.

Zorkoczy, P, 'Teletext systems' in Bates, A W (ed), 1984 (see above).

Section Four. Glossary

Access devices. Means provided by writers to enable the learner to find those parts of the *Chunk* that he needs; *Access devices* include lists of objectives, summaries and self-assessment questions.

Activity. An opportunity to apply learning to the world outside the package.

Affective (used of the curriculum). The area of the curriculum involving feelings, attitudes and emotional responses.

Aim. A general statement of the intention of the planner or writer. See *Goal* and *Objective.*

Assessment. The measurement of learner performance; this may be formal or informal, exact or rough and ready, carried out by the learner himself (self-assessment) or by others. See *Self-assessment question* and *Tutor-assessed question.*

Authoring system/language. A specialized programming language used in creating computer-based packages. An authoring language enables educators, trainers and others to construct CBT programs. Some authoring languages can be used by people without programming experience or knowledge of computing. An authoring language sits within a *System* which provides facilities such as checking and file-handling.

Branching. A term used to describe the process whereby the learner selects one particular option at a point in the learning programme.

Case-study. Presentation of real or imagined experience, often, in an open-learning package, followed by self-assessment questions.

Checklist. A list of questions against which a learner can check progress towards carrying out a particular activity.

Chunk. Part of a package that forms a coherent learning experience; could be short (eg, *Segment)* or longer (eg, *Module)* or at the level of the *Package* as a whole.

Core resource. Text (or equivalent in other media) around which an open-learning package is built.

Course. A planned learning experience. It may be tightly structured (eg, the Open University Undergraduate Programme) or loose (eg, a study circle); it may be long or short in duration; it may or may not lead to a qualification; it may be offered by an educational, industrial or other provider; it may be formal or informal. In industry the word *Programme* is sometimes used instead of *Course.* In this book *Scheme* is used synonymously with *Course.*

Courseware. Learning material developed for use on a computer or computer-controlled system such as interactive video.

Cyclops. Equipment, used mainly within the Open University, which allows a tutor to communicate with remote students via the telephone line. Visual information is

122

displayed on a television screen. The learner can annotate this by using a lightpen. In early systems Cyclops required two telephone lines for visual and audio communication. A more recent modification allows both these forms of communication to be transmitted on one telephone line.

Delivery. The ways in which a *Scheme* provides the learner with materials and support.

Developmental testing. The small-scale try-out of learning materials in draft, on members of the target population. A form of *Pilot.* Cf also *Validation.*

Drop out. A term used to describe the process by which a learner ceases to study within an open-learning scheme. The learner may consciously drop out or just drift into the position of non-contact with the provider.

Editor. An imprecise term for someone with particular responsibility for the package. The editor may have a relatively narrow role (eg, copy-editing) or a very broad one (eg, to issue contracts and train authors). The editor may be responsible for seeing the *House style* is observed, checking technical accuracy and ensuring that the package is designed on sound learning principles. He or she may also supervise the production process, eg, devising and monitoring budgets and schedules.

Evaluation. The process of gathering information from various sources in order to appraise and make decisions about a scheme's effectiveness and worthwhileness. Often used interchangeably with *Monitoring,* but evaluation generally implies a greater degree of detachment and is occasional rather than continuous.

Feedback. The provision of comment on a learner's performance either within the package or by some other means (eg, computer; tutor). In the package this may be called 'answer', 'response' or some similar name.

Firmware. Either the software or courseware held on ROM chip. This allows more rapid access of the software by the computer. It therefore has a status between software (computer programs) and hardware (machinery on which the program is run).

FlexiStudy. An open-learning scheme run by the National Extension College in association with education and training institutions, usually colleges of further education. NEC is the main provider of learning materials and the institution is responsible for support.

Format. The open-learning features used in a package and the way these are shown.

Gateway. A link which allows a *Viewdata* system to access information from an external computer. Such links are transparent to the user. See also *Viewdata, Videotex,* and *Teletext.*

Goal. A more specific statement than an *Aim.* A goal is expressed in terms of learning outcomes but not as specifically as an *Objective.*

HELP section. Part of a *Package* designed to help learners who have got into difficulty.

House style. Instruction given to writers/editors by a publishing organization; the instructions cover such points as which spellings to use, how to record sources. (Sometimes also called 'house rules'.)

Interactive video. Term used to describe the linking of video and computer technologies. At a simple level it involves segmenting videotapes to play selected parts to the learner. At the most sophisticated level it involves full computer control of a videodisc allowing the student to access data, pictures (still or moving) as well as software.

Layout. The way in which words and illustrations are set out on the page or its equivalent (eg, computer screen).

Learner. Anyone learning in an open-learning scheme. In this series 'learner' is chosen as the generic term; cf. 'student', 'trainee', 'employee', 'customer', 'client', 'punter'. All these would be covered by the term 'learner'.

Linear presentation. Presentation of learning material in a sequence which follows on frame by frame or page by page. It implies that there is no branching or learner choice in the way the material is presented.

MAIL. An abbreviation of Micro-Aided Learning, a computerized system developed by the National Extension College in 1983 to provide feedback for open learners.

Maintenance. Action taken to ensure that a *Scheme* continues to run smoothly; servicing a *Scheme*. Both the *Package* and the support system need *Maintenance*.

MARIS. The Materials and Resources Information Service: an Open Tech project managed by the National Extension College for England and Wales and by the Scottish Council for Educational Technology for Scotland.

Medium/media. The means chosen for transmission of the package (eg, audiotape, print).

Microviewdata (sometimes called local viewdata). Software allowing users to create viewdata pages and databases themselves, using a microcomputer. The more sophisticated software packages enable other people to gain access to such databases, via the telephone line. See also *Viewdata*, *Videotex*, and *Teletext*.

Module. A self-contained *Chunk* of learning, part of a *Package*. *Modules* are often between four and 12 hours long. They may themselves be divded into smaller elements (*Segments*). Modular learning materials enable learners to choose which objectives they wish to cover and the sequence in which they wish to cover them. (Note that there is considerable variation between the terms used in different *Schemes* to describe the elements into which a *Course* is divided. For example, instead of *Package*, *Course* may be used; instead of *Module*, 'block' or 'unit'; instead of *Segment*, 'chapter' or 'section'.)

Monitoring. The regular scrutiny of the performance of the scheme, or part of a scheme, as it is running; checking the effectiveness of management procedures, learner support and learning materials with a view to consequent action. Often used interchangeably with *Evaluation*.

Objective. A description of the purpose of a scheme expressed in terms of the capacities that the learner will acquire and demonstrate; a statement of learning outcomes.

Open-learning course/programme/scheme/system. 'Open learning' is a term used to describe courses flexibly designed to meet individual requirements. It is often applied to provision which tries to remove barriers that prevent attendance at more traditional courses but it also suggests a learner-centred philosophy. Open-learning courses may be offered in a learning centre of some kind or most of the activity may be carried out away from such a centre (eg, at home).

OTTSU. The Open Tech Training and Support Unit: an Open Tech project managed by the Council for Educational Technology (see p 24).

Overview. The section at the beginning of a learning sequence which allows the learner to gain a quick insight into what lies before him.

Package/open-learning package/materials/learning materials. Specially prepared or adapted materials that enable the learner to study for a significant part of the time on his own.

Pilot. The trial of a *Scheme* or part of it before full operation, with the intention of collecting feedback, to assess the performance of the scheme and to decide on any modification necessary. Volume 7, *How to Manage the Production Process*, describes two forms of piloting the package; *Developmental testing* and *Validation*.

Post-test. A set of questions that enables the learner to check how successful he has mastered the objectives of a particular *Chunk*.

Practical kit. Any hardware issued for use at home for learning purposes. A kit contains essential components not likely to be found in the home; thus a microscope would be included in a kit but not a pair of scissors.

Pre-test. A series of questions that enables the learner to decide whether or not he needs to study a particular *Chunk* or a part of it.

Program. A series of instructions (usually written in a programming language) which can be understood and obeyed by a computer.

Programme. See *Course*.

Provider/providing body. The institution, organization or individual responsible for making available a particular open-learning scheme (eg, British Telecom, the Open University, Sight and Sound).

Psychomotor (used of the curriculum). The area of the curriculum involving physical skills/manipulation.

Routeing. Guides the learner to appropriate parts of a package and the sequence in which these will be studied.

Scheme. See *Course*.

SCOTTSU. The Scottish Open Tech Training and Support Unit: an Open Tech project managed by Dundee College of Education (see p 26).

Segment. Subdivision of a *Module*.

Self-assessment question (SAQ). An opportunity within the text that enables the learner to prepare for a learning experience; test his understanding of a particular point; enter into dialogue with the package writer.

Self-help group. A group of learners who come together voluntarily to plan and implement a learning programme. Their objectives may be pre-set (eg, a syllabus) or formulated by the learners themselves.

Signposting. Indications of where the learner has got to, come from and is going to; signposting helps the learner to orient himself.

Software. A *Program* or set of *Programs*.

Split screen. A technique whereby the visual display unit or television screen is divided in two, four, or more sections electronically so that different kinds of information can be displayed in each section. Typically text is displayed in one part while a still or moving picture is displayed in another.

Study guide. Material accompanying a *Core resource* (eg, a textbook) providing open-learning features such as *Objectives, Activities* and *Self-assessment questions.*

Support. The arrangements made by an open-learning scheme to provide extra help to the learners to that already contained in the learning package. *Support* includes contact, advice, guidance, counselling, tutoring and the provision of practical experience.

System. See *Open learning course/programme/scheme/system.*

Target audience. The learners for whom a particular course has been prepared; they may be in education (students), training (trainees), work (employees), or others. See *Learner.*

Teleconference. A system whereby any number (up to 15) of telephone lines are linked together in order that a conference call can take place. Each of the participants can hear and speak with all of the other participants. There is usually a voice switching mechanism in the linking bridge which allows only one participant to speak at once.

Telesoftware. A means of storing and distributing materials — software, text and graphics — so that they can be received (downloaded) into the memory of the user's microcomputer through a viewdata or teletext system or over the radio (audio software). These materials can subsequently be stored on disc or cassette.

Teletext. A page-orientated information system using a particular style of frame presentation and transmitted in a fixed cyclical sequence via broadcast signals. These pages are identified by numbers and displayed, as selected, on a special television or a television or microcomputer with an adapter. It is not possible for the user to send information back to such a system. CEEFAX (BBC) and ORACLE (ITV) are examples of teletext systems. See also *Videotex* and *Viewdata.*

Teletext simulator. This is a piece of *Software* which allows a small microcomputer to generate a database of teletext-type pages of information and save these pages on disc.

Teletutoring. Use of the telephone for tutoring as opposed to general support or for the holding of general meetings.

Transformer. Person who turns conventional material into open-learning form.

Tutor. General term for the person in an open-learning system who is directly responsible for the learner. The tutor is usually a professional — an educator or trainer. His main task is to help the learner to acquire skills and strategies needed to become autonomous, usually through mastery of a particular subject area or skill. He is variously described as 'counsellor', 'mentor', 'coach', 'guide', 'trainer', 'supervisor' and 'godfather'.

Tutor-assessed question (TAQ). A question answered by a learner and handed or sent to a tutor for comment and assessment.

Validation. The testing of an open-learning *Package* and/or other components of a *Scheme* in a real context, with a representative sample of the *Target audience.* In practice the words *Validation* and *Pilot* are often used interchangeably. See *Pilot* and *Developmental testing.*

Videotex. The generic term to cover both *Teletext* and *Viewdata.*

Viewdata. An interactive page-orientated computer information storage and retrieval system using a particular style of frame presentation. These pages are stored in a tree structure to form a database. The provision of pages allows information to be easily located. PRESTEL is an example of a viewdata system. See also *Videotex* and *Teletext.*

Workshop/open-learning workshop. An open-learning scheme based in a centre. The learner works in the centre, which holds materials. These can be used by the learner either by dropping in or by booking. (The word *Workshop* is also often used to describe short, participative training events.)

Appendix. Addresses of National Bodies

Appendix. Addresses of National Bodies

These addresses are for organizations mentioned earlier on pp 21–27.

MATERIALS AND RESOURCES INFORMATION SERVICE (MARIS).
MARIS, National Extension College, 1 St Mary Street, Ely, Cambs CB7 4ER.
MARIS Scotland, Scottish Council for Educational Technology, Dowanhill, 74 Victoria Crescent Road, Glasgow G12 9JN.

NATIONAL EXTENSION COLLEGE (NEC)
18 Brooklands Avenue, Cambridge CB2 2HN.

COUNCIL FOR EDUCATIONAL TECHNOLOGY (CET)
3 Devonshire Street, London W1N 2BA.

OPEN TECH TRAINING AND SUPPORT UNIT (OTTSU)
See below, 'Publishers of open-learning materials'.

SCOTTISH COUNCIL FOR EDUCATIONAL TECHNOLOGY (SCET)
Dowanhill, 74 Victoria Crescent Road, Glasgow G12 9JN.

INDUSTRIAL TRAINING BOARDS (ITBS)

Agricultural Training Board
Bourne House, 32/34 Beckenham Road, Beckenham, Kent BR3 4PB.

Clothing and Allied Products Industry Training Board
Tower House, Merrion Way, Leeds LS2 8NY.

Construction Industry Training Board
Radnor House, London Road, Norbury, London SW16 4EL.

Engineering Industry Training Board
St Martins House, 140 Tottenham Court Road, London W1P 9LN.

Hotel and Catering Industry Training Board
PO Box 18, Ramsey House, Central Square, Wembley, Middlesex HA9 7AP.

National Water Council, Training Division
James House, 27 London Road, Newbury, Berks RG13 1JL.

Plastics Processing Industry Training Board
Brent House, 950 Great West Road, Brentford, Middlesex.

Polymer Open Tech
Dowanhill, 74 Victoria Crescent Road, Glasgow G12 9JN.

Road Transport Industry Training Board
Capitol House, Empire Way, Wembley, Middlesex.

NATIONAL TRAINING ORGANIZATIONS
British Association for Commercial and Industrial Education (BACIE)
16 Park Crescent, London W1N 4AP.

Institute of Training and Development (ITD)
5 Baring Road, Beaconsfield, Bucks HP9 2NX.

CORRESPONDENCE COLLEGES
NALGO Correspondence Institute
NALGO House, 1 Mabledon Place, London WC1H 9AJ.

Rapid Results College
Tuition House, 27–37 St George's Road, London SW19 4DS.

Wolsey Hall
66 Banbury Road, Oxford OX2 6PR.

COUNCIL FOR THE ACCREDITATION OF CORRESPONDENCE COLLEGES (CACC)
27 Marylebone Road, London NW1.

OPEN UNIVERSITY
Walton Hall, Milton Keynes, MK7 6AA.

PUBLISHERS OF OPEN-LEARNING MATERIALS
Pan Books Limited
Cavaye Place, London SW10 9PG.

Charles Letts
77 Borough Road, London SE1 1DW.

Tecmedia Limited
5 Granby Street, Loughborough LE11 3DU.

OPEN LEARNING FEDERATION

John Redstone (Chairman), Central Manchester College, St John's Centre, Lower Hardman Street, Manchester M3 3ER.

FURTHER EDUCATION STAFF COLLEGE

Coombe Lodge, Blagdon, Bristol BS18 6RG.

OPEN TECH TRAINING AND SUPPORT UNIT (OTTSU)

Rooms 24–27, Prudential Buildings, Above Bar Street, Southampton SO1 0FG.

OPEN TECH UNIT (OTU)

Manpower Services Commission, Moorfoot, Sheffield S1 4PQ.

SCOTTISH OPEN TECH TRAINING AND SUPPORT UNIT (SCOTTSU)

Dundee College of Education, Gardyne Road, Broughty Ferry, Dundee DD5 1NY.